Pilgrim's Progress

Dedicated to our children's children, hoping that it may accompany them on their life pilgrimages.

To Tovah Zalik-Wallace on her Jewish pilgrimage.

To Jay Preston

To Carmen and Robbie Lansdowne

To Kristopher, Nathan, and Genevieve Allen on their Christian pilgrimages.

Pilgrim's Progress

A Spiritual Guide
for the Holy Land Traveler

Robert and Gwynneth Wallace

Geneva Press
Louisville, Kentucky

Scripture quotations, unless otherwise indicated, are from the New Revised Standard Version of the Bible, copyright © 1989 by the Division of Christian Education of the National Council of the Churches of Christ in the U.S.A., and used by permission.

Psalms quoted by permission from *The Holy Bible, New International Version.* Copyright © 1973, 1978, 1984 International Bible Society. Used by Permission of Zondervan Bible Publishers.

The poem on page 48 is verse three of "We Have Seen His Star" (page 104 *The Poetry of L. M. Montgomery*). Material written by L. M. Montgomery is reproduced here with the permission of David Macdonald, trustee, and Ruth Macdonald, who are the heirs of L. M. Montgomery. *The Poetry of L. M. Montgomery* is published by Fitzhenry & Whiteside, 1987. "L. M. Montgomery" is a trademark of the Heirs of L. M. Montgomery Inc.

Book design by Sharon Adams
Cover design by Night & Day Design
Cover illustration: Dome of the Rock, Jerusalem, Israel. Courtesy of SuperStock.

First published in 1997 by The United Church Publishing House
Reprinted by arrangement with The United Church Publishing House, Canada

First U.S. edition, 2000
Published by Geneva Press
Louisville, Kentucky

This book is printed on acid-free paper that meets the American National Standards Institute Z39.48 standard. ∞

PRINTED IN THE UNITED STATES OF AMERICA

00 01 02 03 04 05 06 07 08 09 — 10 9 8 7 6 5 4 3 2 1

Library of Congress Cataloging-in-Publication Data

Wallace, Robert A. (Robert Arthur), 1928–
   Pilgrim's progress : a spiritual guide for the Holy Land traveler / Robert and Gwynneth Wallace.—1st American ed.
      p.   cm.
   Originally published : Toronto, Ontario : United Church Pub. House, 1997.
   Includes bilbiographical references and index.
   ISBN 0-664-50127-3 (alk. paper)
   1. Israel—Description and travel. 2. Jerusalem—Description and travel. 3. Bible—Geography. 4. Christian pilgrims and pilgrimages—Israel. 5. Devotional calendars. I. Wallace, Gwynneth. II. Title.
DS103.W35 2000
263′.0425694—dc21
                                                                                    99-054012

CONTENTS

FOREWORD

Pilgrim's Progress is written for travelers to the Holy Land, whether they arrive by air or by imagination. It is for tourists and "wannabes," since one can be a pilgrim seated on the back deck as well as on a camel.

This book is designed to supplement other handbooks for travelers by providing the biblical and religious background for exploring Israel. It is intended primarily for personal devotions, but can also be used for group worship.

The sites visited are grouped by regions, moving from Tel Aviv, northward along the coast, inland through Galilee, back to the southern area and finally going up to Jerusalem. We sincerely hope that after traveling in the Holy Land the pilgrim will never read the Bible in the same way again.

Thanks to the United Church Publishing House for suggesting the work, especially Beth Parker, our director of publishing, and Ruth Chernia, our editor. We are grateful to several excellent tour guides in the Holy Land, especially our good friend, Leslie Edwin. The Israel Government Tourist Office has always been helpful.

Our thanks finally to those who have been fellow travelers and walked with us where Jesus walked.

Shalom.

August 1997

INTRODUCTION

The Holy Land is "the fifth gospel," says Sister Jocelyn Monette, a Canadian Sister of Zion in Jerusalem. "The gospel writers assume that we know the topography, geography, and history of Israel."

From snow-capped Hermon in the north to the desolate reaches of parched desert around Gaza, a half-day's travel south, Israel has an amazing terrain. Less than half the size of Nova Scotia, it has three distinct areas, differing not just in the lay of the land but in the way of life. Galilee is green and gentle; the desert severe and forbidding; Jerusalem and Tel Aviv, cosmopolitan, rushed, and noisy. Israel has both busy city streets and vast, empty spaces. It is at once a developed and an undeveloped country.

The love of the Israeli for the land is behind much of the biblical narrative and also much of today's front-page news. Faith in God is tightly bound to the assurance that God intends the Chosen People to inhabit the land promised to Abraham, the land toward which the people trekked with Moses, the land that knew its highest glory under David whose family symbol Israel has emblazoned on its flag today.

Israelis quote the Baal Shem Tov, founder of the Hasidic sect, who wrote "Forgetfulness leads to exile, while remembrance is the secret of redemption." Israel was never forgotten, always remembered.

The Israeli's age-long hopes and dreams assume a God-given right to be in this land. In *The Religions of*

Man,[1] Huston Smith, writes, "It is one of the paradoxes of Judaism that during the two thousand years in which it jumped every national boundary and required no habitation other than the souls of humankind, it retained its passion for the land of its birth."

This is a centuries-long love, exemplified in the life of a young man named Luz, a guide in Jerusalem a hundred years ago. At twenty-three years of age he was told that he would soon be blind. He spent a month standing on rooftops memorizing the city. He continued guiding until he was seventy-three years old, and he wrote forty-three books on Jerusalem!

It is common knowledge that the love of this land causes unrest. The Jew and the Arab each experiences a feeling of encroachment in a land where every square yard is treasured. The high tension between Israel and its neighbors has existed from the first day of Israel's statehood. Geography has shaped and is shaping Israel's history.

In addition, Tel Aviv, Jerusalem, and Haifa, its largest cities, are expanding rapidly, making for crowded conditions. Eighty percent of the population live in apartments.

It takes time and patience to begin unraveling this complex society. The average citizen of Israel is a very intense person. Though Israelis will laughingly say a favorite indoor sport is talking, western visitors often feel an invisible protective wall between themselves and many Israelis.

While Christians may feel kinship with these people who share our Bible, it is harder for the Jew to feel that link. The long history of persecution by Christians means that a Jew must be very tolerant to accept us.

In Israel, there is another world just below your feet. Standing on the Cardo, an unearthed Roman main street in Jerusalem, one can see, in the banks of the excavation, soils from six thousand years of history. A sign in a nearby archaeological project reads, "You have descended three meters below the level of the present Jewish Quarter. You have gone back two thousand years in time."

The pilgrim is grateful for the ambitious and generous program of archaeological excavation undertaken by the State of Israel. Visitors returning after only a year are astonished at the amount of work done in the meantime. Pride in the history of the land is beneficial to all whose faith is rooted in the happenings that took place on this soil.

Mighty God, we look forward to walking in the footsteps of the prophets and priests, heroes and heroines we have known in stories familiar since birth. We wish to walk where Jesus walked, and feel the strength of his presence with us.

Israel—Whose Holy Land?

I am the LORD who brought you from Ur of the Chaldeans, to give you this land to possess.

READ: GENESIS 12:1–4, ISAIAH 9:2–7

No territory in the world has been more contested than the 7,992 square miles (20,700 km²) of the land of Israel. Its conquerors and would-be conquerors include the Egyptians, Assyrians, Babylonians, Persians, Greeks, Romans, Seleucid Turks, Arabs, Seljuks, Crusaders, Mamluks, Ottoman Turks, and British.

They have come and gone, each leaving behind remnants dimly discerned in the multi-layered tells (mounded earth covering a layer-cake of civilizations, one built on the ruins of another) that twentieth-century archaeologists and scholars are exploring.

All this is that land "flowing with milk and honey" promised to the Hebrews, Abraham and his descendants, a promise renewed with Moses and seized on with zeal and holy passion by generation after generation. Through centuries of persecution and flight, the exiled Jews of the Diaspora lived out the promise each Seder meal, concluding the commemoration with the words, "Next year in Jerusalem."

Finally, in 1948 the dream came true. Jews from all over the world flooded into the newly constituted State of Israel. In 1950 legislation was passed declaring that anyone who could claim Jewish heritage was a welcome immigrant.

Another world faith also sees Jerusalem as holy ground. The Dome of the Rock, with the Al Aqsa mosque by its side, dominates the skyline of Jerusalem and the wail of the muezzin calling Muslims to prayer reminds the traveler that for nearly thirteen centuries most of the inhabitants of the Holy Land were followers of Mohammed. So are most Arab and Palestinian residents in Israel today. Tenants of the Islamic faith require Moslems to visit and venerate holy places. They regard the height of land crowned by the golden dome in Jerusalem as "the center of the earth," the point from which Mohammed made a night journey to the heavens to receive the Koran. Much of the tension in the city revolves around the fact that three major faiths venerate this shrine.

Israel is also home to the Baha'i faith with its world center in Haifa. Abba Eban calls Israel "the cradle of faiths and the testing ground of creeds."

Christians visit the Holy Land not merely as tourists, but as pilgrims. Pilgrimage is a meeting place of visitor, the land, and the divine. Pilgrimage in the Holy Land was a major component of the devout life in the early years of Christianity. The Empress Helena, mother of Constantine the Great, traveled throughout the Holy Land in the fourth century and, as she designated holy sites and built churches, she set a pattern for pilgrimage.

Early guides for Christian pilgrimage promoted a penitential attitude. The emphasis has shifted to evocation, prayer, and contemplation. Standing on hallowed ground the pilgrim visualizes scenes from scripture that are the foundation of faith.

Christians encounter patriarchs and places familiar since childhood, walk where Jesus and his followers most surely walked, stand surrounded by stones that shout his name. New Testament women emerge, powerful voices heralding Jesus as Messiah.

At traditional holy places, pilgrims marvel at the ornamentation that makes a place "holy" for fellow Christians from unfamiliar denominations. Greek and Russian Orthodox, Armenian, Syrian, Copt decorate in a way that is at once strange and yet familiar. With awe, the pilgrim comes to the recognition that "This is *my own* Holy Land."

This is the Holy Land for all who can go beyond the contradictions and complexities of modern Israel to come home to the presence of God. "This year in Jerusalem."

Lord God of Abraham and Sarah, Rebecca, Leah, and Isaac, we rejoice that we stand in the line of succession to receive from you a Holy Land, a land that renews our faith through the memory of strong words and powerful deeds. May each encounter with that land deepen our ties with your son, Jesus Christ.

*T*el Aviv

*From one ancestor God made all nations
to inhabit the earth.*

READ: ACTS 17:22–31, GALATIANS 3:23–29

Tel Aviv, meaning "Hill of Spring," is not a likely destination for pilgrims, but it boasts Israel's only international airport, which means that thousands of pilgrims pass through Tel Aviv on their way to "seeing what their hearts feel."

For Jews it may be a business trip or a visit to family—"I come twice a year to visit my daughter on the kibbutz." Others come to fulfill a cherished dream, "Next year in Jerusalem!" Many feel that here, with the Chosen People, as nowhere else, they can worthily worship Adonai.[2]

Muslim pilgrims head for the Temple Mount to fulfill a long-held dream of visiting the shrine of the Dome of the Rock, from where, in a vision, Mohammed journeyed to heaven to receive the Koran, and praying in Al Aqsa mosque. They will reap a spiritual reward, for Allah grants a blessing on this pilgrimage.

The Christian pilgrims come to worship God as revealed in his son, Jesus Christ, who lived in this land and whose life can be traced across the holy sites.

Expectations run high in this airport. Security is

tight. Israel wishes safe passage for its pilgrims! A sign outside reads, "Shalom, hurry back. We miss you already."

It is just an hour to Jerusalem. Ninety percent of Israel's population live within an hour and a half of Ben Gurion airport. The population lives in a small space geographically and psychologically.

Tel Aviv is a new city, on the Mediterranean shore, sometimes referred to as the New York of the Middle East. Denied immigration for centuries, by 1909 Jews from Europe began filtering back to settle in the suburbs of ancient Joppa (now Jaffa), bringing with them buildings and businesses in western style. Now the Jaffa market and galleries and chic modern restaurants with a Mediterranean view beckon visitors.

The Museum of the Diaspora is a "must see," particularly for first time visitors. Located on the grounds of Tel Aviv University, it is dedicated to understanding the Jews and their scattered lives. In multimedia presentations one is introduced to Jewish life in eighty countries where more than a hundred languages are spoken. The distinction between Sephardic and Ashkanazi Jews is made clear and travelers are introduced to Jewish art and culture.

Tel Aviv helps one make the transition as pilgrims become immersed in a fascinating land that yields its mysteries to those who are questioning and receptive. It is well to be rested and prepared.

God of all lands, we thank you for this land with all that it means to so many of your people. May it bring a deepening of faith and a new appreciation for the faith of others.

Joppa

*This is the day that the Lord has made;
let us rejoice and be glad in it.*

READ: JONAH 1:3–17, ACTS 10:1–23

Joppa (or Yaffa) is thirty-six hundred years old, probably the oldest port in the world. Its narrow, winding passageways, musty antique and curio shops, and galleries lure the visitor. Evening dinner on a patio overlooking the harbor and the legendary Rock of Andromeda is a treat. The ancient harbor, where the cedars of Lebanon were unloaded for the building of Solomon's temple, is the perfect place to begin a Christian pilgrimage. It looks as we expect the Holy Land to look.

More important, its biblical significance provides a starting place for the spirit of exploration. This is the port from which Jonah shipped out to escape God's request that he preach to the people of Nineveh. To minister to strangers, or worse, to enemies, was unthinkable. The effigy of the whale on Joppa's waterfront is a reminder of the means God used to bend Jonah to his will.

Much later the disciple Peter came to Joppa and healed a young woman thought dead. While staying in the house of Simon the Tanner, he had a vision of animals that represented meat ritually "unclean," forbidden. In the vision he was told to eat. Later, when subordinates of a Roman military ruler came to Joppa, asking Peter to come and heal the official's daughter, he realized that the vision had released him to preach to Gentiles. The early church was ready to move beyond its restrictive origins.

Peter and Jonah were each given, in a mystic manner, a ministry to break down barriers, to open sealed borders, to reach out beyond the familiar with respect and openness. Jonah resisted, but finally obeyed. Peter, in a courageous about-face, admitted that he had been narrow in his judgment and he opened the young church to the world beyond the Jewish people. Joppa became a place of openness to new beginnings.

Looking out where the Mediterranean lashes at the seawall, one can almost see Peter the fisherman walking on the rock-bound shore. He is wondering what it means to be a "fisher of men." Twenty-two Joppa churches named for Peter are witnesses to the answer he found.

Eternal God, you who have made of one blood all the nations of the earth. We travel among people whose languages are different from our own, whose faiths are foreign to us, whose ways we often do not understand. Keep us open to your spirit in words of truth, in works of beauty, in actions that heal, wherever they are found. We pray in the name of Christ, who called us to be good neighbors. Amen.

Caesarea

Blessed is the one who walks in the way of the Lord.

READ: ACTS 12:18–24

Herod the Great, responsible for so much of the impressive building seen in the Holy Land, created in Caesarea on opulent but thoroughly Roman seat of government. As a counterweight to Jewish Jerusalem with its harbor in Joppa, he added an ingenious breakwater and inner harbor. The blue-green Mediterranean waters still lap on the stony harbor remnants.

Herod also built an aqueduct, an engineering marvel, to bring water six miles from Mount Carmel. Travelers can climb the ancient structure that still rises above the sand and walk along the sand-filled conduits. Photographers use the semi-circular arches to frame shots of the Mediterranean.

In Jesus' day Pontius Pilate lived in Caesarea. From here he journeyed to Jerusalem for Passover and for the trial of Jesus. Visitors view a stone bearing his name, unearthed in recent excavating.

Christians may recall Caesarea as the scene of Peter's conversion of a Roman centurion and also the place of Paul's imprisonment and embarkation for

Rome. There is, however, another significant story directly related to the fine Roman amphitheater.

Soon after the death of Jesus, Herod Aggripus I became Governor. He was a close friend of Roman Emperor Caligula and shared with him a detestation of the Christian sect. It was in the amphitheater that still stands that he made a violent speech condemning his enemies. Then amidst shouts of flattering adulation he collapsed and died. The Bible speaks of his being struck down by an angel of the Lord! Pilgrims can sit in the royal box and imagine the scene.

Soon afterward Caligula was assassinated. The Christian church, small and fragile at this point in its growth, might easily have been crushed by these despots. Instead the church flourished, even in Caesarea. Ironically, it was from Herod's port that Paul sailed to Rome bringing Christianity to the foremost city of the ancient world. A few centuries later this lovely seaport city was home for one of the early church's most influential theologians, Origen, whose library has recently been excavated by archaeologists.

The remnants of this ancient and majestic city, the theater, the royal box, even Paul's prison (recently excavated) stand on its sandy shore, a symbol of the providential life and growth of Christ's church.

Eternal God, your will for us is shown in men and women of courage through the centuries. But here, in this awesome place, we are humbled by the power of faithfulness of those who have stood their ground confident in your powerful presence. May our own faith sustain the lighter blows of scorn or apathy with equal assurance.

Akko

How lonely sits the city that was full of people.

READ: HAGGAI 1:7–9, LAMENTATIONS 1:1–16, ACTS 21:7

The crusades were undertaken by western European Christians between 1075 and 1270. They were motivated by dreams of adventure, religious fervor, and the belief that they were following the will of God. In fact, rewards offered were remission of sins, expiation of penance, an assured place in heaven, and all the booty one could plunder! Crusaders (cross carriers) set off at the behest of the papacy to reclaim the Holy Land from the Muslims who were overthrowing the Byzantine Empire.

To establish and maintain a Christian presence, some of the crusading armies remained in the Holy Land, building castles and fortresses and replacing Arab mosques with Christian churches. Although some of the leaders were of noble birth and many were devout; others, untrained for leadership, were unprincipled, barbaric despots who ruled ruthlessly.

Five years after the conquest of Jerusalem, following a two-year siege and the loss of eighty thousand people, the ancient city of Akko (or Acre) became the crusader capital. It was the headquarters of the Knights of the Hospital of St. John (the Hospitallers), a religious and military order of knights associated with St. Augustine, who protected pilgrims and cared for the sick. (The modern St. John Ambulance Brigade was founded by the revived order.) The monumental subterranean crusader city of Akko is wonderfully preserved. The majestic halls, with vaulted ceilings, gigantic rooms with paved stone floors, an immense refectory, and long "secret tunnels," have been unearthed below an eighteenth-century citadel. This archaeological wonder, rescued from mountains of earth and sand, has been excavated with care in order to preserve carefully the integrity of the mighty citadel above it.

Akko flourished as a densely populated port and trading center. Churches were erected but fell into decay with the advent of Arab occupation in the thirteenth century.

Crusaders returning to their homelands were traditionally buried as portrayed on their tombs, with arms and feet crossed, a sign that they had fought for the cross. Could it be that to this day we seek the ancient mystique when we keep our fingers crossed?

Many crusaders traveled east with sincerely devout motives. They made astonishing sacrifices to accomplish their goal of "liberating" the Holy Land. Many masked greed and prejudice (especially toward Jews), under the guise of piety. The trail of carnage they left in their wake is an example of how easily the finest intentions can be warped by foolishness, hostility, and lust.

O God, give us eyes to see clearly your truth in life's complexity. Then may we be freed from the temptation to cloak our selfish desires in words of piety or deeds of charity.

Carmel

How long will you go limping between opinions? If God be God, then follow him.

READ: 1 KINGS 18 (KEY VERSES 20–39)

Haifa is a busy seaport city and commercial center with Mount Carmel rising above the city like a large and comforting shoulder. Haifa's most striking feature is the grandeur of the golden domed Baha'i shrine part way up the mountain, its terraced gardens gradually taking the form and color of a Persian carpet. Pilgrims are welcomed by gracious hosts at the shrine, and can visit the picture-perfect gardens above the emerald Mediterranean.

It is not so much the modern city of Haifa that engages the pilgrim, however, as the mountain top. From here one sees commercial Haifa on one side and on the other the green and fertile Jezreel Valley, site of much Old Testament history. Here a Carmelite Monastery is built on the site of Elijah's contest with the prophets of Baal. An impressive statue of fiery Elijah greets pilgrims entering the monastery grounds.

On a promontory overlooking the valley as it stretches out toward Galilee, Elijah, alone and lonely, yet confident in God's call, defended the faith given to the children of Israel. He challenged the powerful forces of a pagan religion marshaled by Queen

Jezebel, a truly formidable female. The account is one of the most dramatic in the Bible, full of surprises, daring dialogue, and human irony. The detail is rich and wondrous, but the main point is supremely important. Under royal sponsorship the nation was being threatened with a faith that rivaled that of Moses and the laws of Adonai.

Phoenician Queen Jezebel brought with her belief in magic and in the need to placate the gods. The foundation of Baal worship was the power of proper ritual to bring about prosperity and success. Sacred prostitutes and bizarre fertility rites were a part of the luxury and vice of her cult. These observances combined to create a culture of decadence that threatened to drain the moral vitality of Israel.

It all seemed innocent enough in good times—simple sacrifices of fruit, grain, and animals to appease Baal. But in times of crisis, such as drought, more drastic action was required. Human sacrifice was not unknown.

Elijah saved faith in Adonai from extinction and his dramatic success earned him a special place in Judaism. It carried him over into the New Testament where he is ranked with Moses. It is said that he will come again as forerunner to the Messiah.

Preserve us, O God, from all the beckoning faiths that surround us, offering an easy way to fullness of life. Give us a daring spirit that holds tenaciously to the good news of your coming in Jesus Christ.

Megiddo

From everlasting to everlasting you are God.

READ: 2 KINGS 23:28–30, JUDGES 5:19–21,
REVELATION 16:12–16

James A. Michener's best-seller *The Source* contains countless personalities, but the one central element in the lengthy novel is "the tell," "the best tell in the country," according to one of his characters. From Michener, a whole generation learned this archaeological term for the barren elliptical mounds, with smooth even sides and flattened tops, evident in many parts of Israel. A scale model at the Megiddo museum assists in understanding the excavation.

The Source tells the story of the fictional "Tell Makor," but the prototype for the narrative is Tell Megiddo, probably the most famed excavation site in the Holy Land. Central to Michener's narrative was the astonishing engineering feat that saw an ancient people tunnel 180 feet (55 m) deep below their city and out another 360 feet (110 m) to a water source beyond the walls. The traveler is not long in Israel before the crucial importance of water is clear. Day trips begin with securing bottled water for the journey. The "water of life" is indeed a vivid New Testament image.

At Megiddo archaeologists have identified twenty

separate cities built one upon another over the centuries. Many bloody battles were fought in this locality. The last was the crucial defeat of the Turkish Empire in 1918 by British forces commanded by E. H. H. Allenby (later Lord Allenby of Megiddo) headquartered here. The word Megiddo has become a term for warfare, including the final cosmic battle between good and evil at the end of time—Armageddon (Mount Megiddo).

Megiddo is the most strategic real estate in Israel. Possession of this height of land meant control of the Via Maris, the road to the sea, the silk and spice trade route from Egypt and Syria. Solomon fortified Megiddo and made it a chariot city. Remains of his stables are evident in the digs.

Conqueror after conqueror subdued and occupied the stone cities that toppled on one another to create this mystic mound. Races and peoples follow one another in dazzling diversity. One prays that the twenty civilizations buried in Tell Megiddo may, in God's good time, be crowned by humanity that will finally have learned to live in peace.

Eternal One, our minds range over ages past, through the tangled tale of human history, and with awe we know that you were present from the beginning and will be present until the end. In this we find confidence and comfort, for you are a God of forgiveness and hope.

Nazareth

*In the sixth month the angel Gabriel was sent from
God to a city of Galilee named Nazareth.*

READ: LUKE 1:26–35, 4:16–22

Nazareth, tucked among green, softly rolling hills, was
a small city, far from centers of trade, when a young
Mary, drawing water from the spring-fed town well,
heard the time-shattering words of the angel Gabriel,
"Hail favored one, blessed of women." The words that
followed, the "Annunciation," the announcement of
the Messiah's coming, changed Nazareth forever.

Today Nazareth is still a small, unpretentious city.
Travelers are drawn to the lofty Church of the Annunciation with its dome that rises like a modern
lighthouse, representing Christ the Light of the World.
Built by the Franciscans in 1968, it is the work of
famed Italian architect Giovanni Muzio, and in it is a
collection of fine ecclesiastical art, much of it devoted
to the Virgin Mary. Though Christians are a minority
in this Arab community, there are eighteen churches
of the Annunication!

In the Orthodox Church of St. Gabriel, an opening
in the floor allows a view of the spring from which
the population have drawn water for three thousand
years. The water supplies a well that tradition cites as
the place of encounter between Mary and the angel.

The holy and humdrum are found side by side as one strolls through the narrow, winding alleys of the market, the air sweet with almond blossom. Merchants advertise wares as they have done for centuries. Flowing gowns for Arab women hang alongside freshly butchered lamb. Buns and baklava are piled precipitously on baker stalls. There is a fragrance of roasted sesame as an erect young Arab passes with a tray of hot pastry rings balanced on his head.

Inside a fenced courtyard the pilgrim finds a well-preserved, ancient synagogue. Though renovated and reshaped over the centuries, it is very likely that the voice of Jesus once echoed here, "The Spirit of the Lord is upon me . . ." It is one of the moments treasured by pilgrims who feel their feet touch the very stones that Jesus walked.

Yet this is, above all, the city of Mary, the mother. One sees scarlet lilies, Mary's flower, nodding at the side of the street. The lily may also be the root meaning of the name, Nazareth. One thinks of the young woman, betrothed but unmarried responding, "Behold, all generations shall call me blessed." And blessed are we that she would listen and respond.

Holy Jesus, we are grateful for this place of encounter where the life of all humanity took new shape.
Blessed is Mary, and blessed are we whose lives have been made whole by your birth.

Sepphoris

*And Jesus increased in wisdom and stature and in
favor with God and man. (KJV)*

READ: MARK 6:1–6

Recent excavations in the Galilee have unearthed the
city of Sepphoris, known for its elegance as "The Jewel
of the Galilee." Designed as the Roman capital of the
Galilee, it enshrined the best of Greco-Roman culture.
As well as being a well-defended governing city, Sepphoris had theaters, reception and meeting halls, and
centers of learning.

The pilgrim can stroll a colonnaded Roman street
and recline on the triclineum where the ancient Romans would have lounged to eat and drink. Excavations have exposed extensive tiled floors and superb
mosaics preserved by drifting sand from destruction
by the bright Galilee sun. Based on Greek myths, they
are striking in detail and shading. On one mosaic
floor is a female face so exquisite in design that it is
referred to as the Mona Lisa of the Galilee.

After only sixteen years as capital the administra-
tion was transferred to Tiberias and Sepphoris lost
some of its luster. Much later it became a crusader
headquarters. From their fortress, remarkably preserved, they marched out to crushing defeat.

Not mentioned in the Bible, Sepphoris was just a

two-hour walk from Nazareth. In Nazareth, off the trade routes, people lived a simple life. To "see the world" one could walk to Sepphoris. Jesus, a builder more likely in stone than in wood, would have found this grand city of hewn stone of immense interest.

Ancient Galilee is often caricatured as a first century backwater, but its trade centers generated a thriving economy and close contact with traders from Egypt, Syria, and Babylon, creating a cosmopolitan and sophisticated population. While people lacked the scholastic pursuits of Jerusalem they had a healthy combination of worldliness and a stern morality that must have influenced Jesus' ministry.

In this cosmopolitan setting one can imagine that he may even have attended the open-air theater. Jesus occasionally used words that have a Greco-Roman slant. One of these was his use of the word "hypocrite." His use of it is similar to our own, but scholars believe that the word was not in such general use at the time. It was a theater term, referring to one acting a part.

Could it be that some of his capacity to deal with people from many ways of life began in his brush with the cultured life of Sepphoris?

God of all ages and all peoples, we are grateful for all who have created beauty; for those who have, with delicacy of touch, turned stone to graceful columns, for those who have left the record of their time in line and color for all who come after.

Cana

*Jesus and his disciples were also invited
to the wedding.*

READ: JOHN 2:1–12

Imagine Jesus at a wedding reception. Picture him sitting with the guests listening to the spirited retelling of village gossip, nodding at the boring tales often heard, feeling uncomfortable with the poor taste that often accompanies such conversation, feeling hopefulness at the beginning of a new family life.

The little hill-town of Cana stands as a symbol of Jesus' gracious willingness to participate in the mundane life of human community. It is apparent from other references in scripture that Jesus knew the town. Cana may be our best earthly reminder of God's willingness to be "incarnate," to enter fully into our commonplace human scene.

Soft hills surround Cana, and green orchards press against its boundaries. The simple red-roofed Franciscan church houses an earthen pitcher from the time of Jesus' life and the altar mural depicts the miracle of water into wine. (Some Christians in generations past might have preferred a reversal of the miracle!)

The by-play between Jesus and his mother is fascinating. While he remains respectful, he hints at the separation, even isolation, that his missions will bring. At the same time, once he has established his independence, he responds to her request.

Meanwhile his mother, dimly aware of his divine nature, quietly supports his first public acts of revelation. Jesus' presence and his participation indicate his approval of the institution of marriage and, for the Roman Catholic Church, his action in Cana validates marriage as a formal sacrament.

Today affable merchants are happy to continue the tradition of Cana as the wedding town by selling pilgrims "wedding wine" to take home for the next appropriate occasion.

Like so many sites in Galilee this town evokes contemplation about the life of Jesus and its meaning for us. These visits recall stories familiar from childhood. One visualizes anew scenes that are a foundation of faith. The heady air of the hills may well provide the same sense of exhilaration, intoxication of the spirit, that Jesus' own presence brought to the little gathering at that long-ago wedding feast.

Gracious God, we thank you for the way in which Jesus blessed a simple celebration by his presence and by his warm concern for the festive party. We thank you for occasions of mirth and merriment, for friendship and festivity. In our time in this land may we draw strength and nourishment from laughter and lighthearted friendship as we talk and travel together, as we sing and celebrate. We pray in the name of Jesus who enlivened the wedding feast so long ago.

The Sea of Galilee

*Then Jesus, filled with the power of the Spirit,
returned to Galilee.*

READ: MARK 4:35–41, LUKE: 5:1–7, MATT. 4:18–22

Is it a lake or is it a sea? It is the only fresh water body
in the Middle East. The desert people of biblical times
had no word for "lake" but they did know the sea,
hence the ancient misnomer for the 14 mile (23 km)
by 8 mile (13 km) harp-shaped "Sea of Galilee," also
called Kinneret, Genessaret, and the Sea of Tiberias.
The sparkling water is completely encircled by beach
with high escarpments on the east and southwest and
terraced plains on the north and northwest. On its
southward course the River Jordan flows through the
lake and ends in the Dead Sea.

The clear, cold lake contained many fish in the
time of Jesus. Catching, preserving, and marketing
fish was a leading occupation.

Jesus knew this lake. He also knew fishermen,
boats, nets, and even how to cook fish! Here the pilgrim is offered a traditional meal of St. Peter's fish, a
spiny, scaly delicacy, a favorite in Galilean restaurants.

Storms occur on the lake at any season and there
are a few places where change comes rapidly. *The
Dictionary of Christ and the Gospels* says that "the
storms on the Sea of Galilee are in many ways pecu-

liar. Sometimes the wind seems to blow from various directions at one time tossing a boat around. Winds blow violently down the gorges and strike the sea at an angle, stirring the waters to great depth."[3] Sudden local storms can turn the glassy surface to dangerous foam-crested waves. Twice it is recorded that Jesus dealt with the capricious nature of the lake startling his disciples with, "Peace. Be still."

Political tensions existed then as now. To "cross the lake" eastward was politically unwise, as several areas were unfriendly or even hostile to the Jews. "Crossing the lake" meant moving the length of the lake along neutral shores.

Near Tagbah the shore takes on an unusual formation that suggests the shape of an amphitheater. In this locale acoustics are such that the spoken word can be heard high in the surrounding hills. Many believe that this is where Jesus preached from a boat "pushed out from the shore" to avoid the press of the crowds.

Josephus, first-century historian, reports that there were 240 cities and villages in the Galilee. It is hard to imagine this serene and quiet countryside with its newly developed drip-irrigated agriculture as a bustling center of trade, influenced by Romans, Greeks, and caravaners from the east! This lake, this region, was Jesus' country. This spirit prevails.

Christ Jesus, may we learn your "Peace, be still."

Galilean Towns

He went down to Capernaum, a city in Galilee . . .

The Galilee makes up one third of Israel. The Syrian-African rift ruptures the landscape, producing broken hills and valleys in which no straight roads are possible.

In Jesus' time there were 240 communities in the Galilee. Josephus, the Jewish historian, writes, "The cities lie very thick, and are so populous that the very least of them contains more than 15,000 inhabitants." There were trails and roads everywhere. It was busy! The mountain air was invigorating and the people of the Galilean highland were vigorous and independent.

The pilgrim discovers a different Galilee. Only Tiberias ranks as a city of note and most of the place names familiar from the gospels have disappeared or are tiny hamlets. Magdala is an example. If Jesus followed the natural route from Nazareth to the Lake of Galilee, this town of Mary Magdalene was probably his first preaching point in Galilee. He would have found a busy fishing center, with over 250 boats, dye works, and a textile trade. Today, as tour buses pass, guides merely gesture toward a tumbled down collection of dwellings in the midst of a dusty palm grove.

Nearby, in a hilly natural amphitheater, the probable site of the Sermon on the Mount, is a modern church. Its octagonal shape represents the eight beatitudes. Below, on the shore, another church marks the site of the feeding of the five thousand. It contains one of the Holy Land's treasures, the loaves and fishes in the simple and bold lines of a primitive mosaic. Nearby, the risen Christ prepared breakfast for his friends.

Chorazim, a town mentioned only once in the gospels, is shrouded in mystery, with echoes of wonders and shadows of failure. Its fine archaeological site high above the lake on a windswept mountain plain shows evidence of an impressive town, with fine Roman architecture in gleaming basalt. It was a production center for drying fish, a town renowned for its fine grain crops, the site of a graceful synagogue. Toward the end of his Galilean ministry Jesus spoke sadly, saying, "Woe to you Chorazim . . ." saying that if he had done such mighty works elsewhere people would have followed, but the people of Chorazim were apparently unmoved. The pilgrim feels the sense of pathos and loss looking over what must have once been a cherished community.

God of the ages, our minds reach back to that small group of earliest followers who stood on the shore and listened with awe and hopefulness to the words of authority that lifted their lives to a brave new level of purpose. The voice is gone, the words remain. Open our ears, we pray.

Tiberias

Boats from Tiberias came near the place where they had eaten the bread . . .

READ PSALM 119:1–16

It is unlikely that Jesus taught in Tiberias, although his Galilean ministry took place nearby. During his ministry, Jesus avoided Roman cities. He was eighteen when the cornerstone of Tiberias was laid. An ancient Jewish settlement was being transformed into a major Roman center, famous for the thermal springs and baths that infatuated the Romans!

The steep hills that rise above Tiberias deflect the Mediterranean breezes that cool much of the Galilee. This city, 700 feet (216 m) below sea level, becomes too hot and humid to endure in the summer. In earlier days malaria threatened the population. In the last century one traveler described it as "a picture of disgusting filth and frightful wretchedness." Today it is a flourishing resort, its streets lined with palm trees. Remnants of the past—crusader castles, an ancient seawall all set in lush gardens and greenery—line the shore of the Sea of Galilee that sparkles in the sunlight. It is an ideal central location for touring the Galilee.

While Tiberias has no place in early Christian history it is revered by the Jews as one of four holy cities of Judaism. (The others are Jerusalem, Safed, and Hebron). It is venerated for the Jewish religious teachers, who, for eight centuries after the Jews were banished from Jerusalem, lived and worked here in academies of biblical study (yeshivas). Here major contributions were made to the Mishna and the Palestinian Talmud, the authoritative writings on Jewish law.

It is essential for Christians who wish to read the Old Testament intelligently to be aware that "the law" for the religious Jew is not merely rules and regulations but *the* way of life that brings one close to God.

Among the most helpful interpreters of the Law in Tiberias were men like Rabbi Akkiba and Moses Maimonides whose tombs are visited by Jewish pilgrims. Maimonides, a twelfth-century philosopher and physician, often referred to as "the second Moses," explained the law in such helpful terms that he is still revered as an interpreter of the Jewish faith. In his "Eight Principles of Charity" he describes the least form of charity as the one in which the donor makes a speech, and the best when the donor employs people even if it causes him a loss! His burial place in the heart of the city is marked by a soaring, red, flame-like sculpture above his tomb. "The flame of God is the spirit of man."

Creator of all, you have gifted us with men and women of keen mind, compassionate spirit, and charitable will. We give thanks for all such persons, especially those whose memories bless this land.

Capernaum

*As he was walking along Jesus saw Levi . . . sitting at
the tax booth, and he said to him, "Follow me." And
he got up and followed him.*

READ: MARK 2:1–17

The ruins of a clearly identifiable synagogue are set
among waving palms and, in the spring and early
summer, their lines are softened with purple
bougainvillea and blowing red poppies. It is a fourth-
century structure built, almost certainly, over the site
of the synagogue in which Jesus preached. Here pilgrims pause to recall that Capernaum was the center
of Jesus' life for almost two years as he began his ministry of preaching, teaching, and healing. It was here
that his first disciples lived and Peter's home, now sur-
mounted by a boat-shaped Franciscan chapel, was a
second home to Jesus himself.

Here Jesus healed Peter's mother-in-law, the centurion's servant, the palsied man let down through the
roof, two blind men, and many more. Here he raised
from the dead the daughter of Jarius, a synagogue
leader.

Why Capernaum? There are many reasons. It was
the home of good friends. It was a large, wealthy, and
influential commercial center on the Sea of Galilee
with a Roman garrison. One of the great trade routes
of Asia Minor, the Via Maris, from the Mediterranean

to Damascus and Egypt ran just above this toll-gate city. Indigents, first-century "street people," from the whole of the Galilee migrated to the pleasant, moderate winter climate of Capernaum and dispersed in the desperate summer heat. This location with its tide of travelers, provided Jesus with a flood of listeners who told and retold what they had seen and heard.

"Nothing is by chance" says one commentator of Jesus' choice of Capernaum. The word Capernaum, means "City of Nahum." Nahum was regarded as the prophet to the Gentiles. Jesus required some rabbinical authority to justify preaching to those outside the Jewish faith. Capernaum was a logical choice because of its association with a prophetic voice from the past who dared to reach beyond the bounds of Judaism.

As we stand on ground hallowed by time and history we reflect on the possibility that even our own presence is not by "chance." God intends a refreshing and renewing of our spirits and we rejoice in this time of illumination for our faith.

Great God of the Ages, your purposes run like a mighty life-giving stream through all human history. We believe that your purposes flow through the years of our lives also. We are grateful for this startling meeting with our Lord, Jesus Christ. We pray that we may be inspired as those who walked among the stones that still stand in place, blessed by his presence.

Caesarea Philippi

You are the Messiah, the Son of the living God!

READ: MATTHEW 16:13–20

There are two major rivers in Israel. The main river, known and sung about by Christians around the world, flows crystal clear and pure from headwaters near ancient Caesarea Philippi. The stony banks afford a firm footing for pilgrims to collect Jordan water to carry home for baptisms!

Later this place was called Banias, after the Greek god Pan. Tradition designates a dark cave here as the home of Pan. Pan was a strange contradiction, on one hand the god of flocks and shepherds, of agriculture and farmers, and protector of nature; on the other, a wild and disturbing lecher whose startling appearance gives us the word "panic."

Jesus and his band had withdrawn from the turbulence surrounding his ministry in Galilee, and were retreating in this mystical craggy location. Peter, overcome with the awesome surroundings, blurted out the conviction that had been growing within him, "You are the Christ, the son of the living God!" Jesus, as he so often did, used the context to color his response. "Simon, your faith is the rock on which I will build my church!"

The Greek biographer Plutarch tells of a mariner on the Mediterranean hearing a voice calling out three times, "When you get to port proclaim that the great god Pan is dead." The date that Plutarch gives to the incident is the exact time period in which the Christian church was taking root in Israel. A strange story, but one that somehow relates to the vision of a faith that would bring order to the world rather than panic, compassion rather than exploitation.

Not far from Banias, the headwaters of this all-important water source are on the other side of the border within Syria, a mismatch in arbitrary border setting! The water supply is a point of contention and division between neighboring states. The pilgrim strolling the lovely park area around Banias, or walking the short distance down the river to a soothing waterfall, finds hope for an acceptable solution knowing that it was in this peaceful setting that the dream was born that Jesus of Nazareth would be proclaimed Lord of Lords and King of Kings and would reign forever and ever.

Strong Spirit of God, you move in a mysterious way to shape the story of our human race on earth. May the clear waters of mountain rivers and the cleansing wind that caresses the trees bring us freedom from all panic or despair. May the coming of the Christ be the source of hopefulness and confidence in a life that can often be tense and fearful.

Safed

Happy are those who delight in God's commandments.

READ: PROVERBS 1:1–7

Jesus said, "A city set on a hill cannot be hid." Safed is certainly set on several hills, as the traveler will know after a half-hour torturous bus ride up hairpin turns to the summit of the highest city in Israel. Perhaps Jesus, preaching in lakeshore Capernaum directly below, gestured upward toward Safed to illustrate. As well as being the nation's highest city it is one of its most picturesque.

In Jesus' day it was a tiny village, not mentioned in the New Testament. Soon afterward the Romans built here. Within a century it achieved fame as a center of Jewish biblical study. The city retained this character through crusader and Turkish domination until the sixteenth century, when rabbinical scholarship flourished so powerfully that it was designated one of the four holy cities of Judaism.

This report arose from its association with an intensive study of scripture that attaches hidden meanings to every letter and number. Only those initiated into the secret meaning can read the Torah with the greatest depth of understanding. This school of thought, the Kabbala, originated in Safed and nearby Meron. Safed is revered for the memory of its distinguished scholars. Devout Jews come from all over the world to pay homage at the tombs of these renowned men and so to receive a blessing.

The pilgrim will find a visit to some of the ancient synagogues of Safed a fascinating experience. One finds a way through the narrow, twisting hillside streets to the Sephardic synagogue of Joseph Caro with its ornate decor. Then on to the vaulted roof and olive-wood carved Torah shrine in the Ashkenazi Ha'ari synagogue. It is instructive to feel the different ethos in the buildings that represent the two strains of Jewish life.

With its cool air and its incredible view, Safed also has been a popular summer resort as well as a center for devotion. Consequently it has always been popular with artists. At one time there was a multitude of galleries. Due to the increasing presence of Orthodox Judaism, the art colony is on the wane but it still provides an afternoon of browsing.

Christian pilgrims come away with renewed respect for the dedication to learning that typifies Judaism. A visit to a local yeshiva, a school of biblical study, confirms the impression. Students choose a study partner for life since they believe that learning must be social. There is only one door to the yeshiva because "there is no exit"—learning scripture is a lifelong process.

In the beginning was the word, and you, God, are that word. May we never neglect the study of your word, for in it is life and life eternal.

Nablus

He came to a Samaritan city named Sychar . . .
Jacob's well was there . . .

READ: GENESIS 12:6–9, JOHN 4:1–30

Jesus' long conversation with the Samaritan woman took place at Jacob's well, near Nablus. Located on the eastern slope of Mount Gerazim, the well stands beside a Greek Orthodox church, the latest of several built to mark the site. The soft rolling hills of the region have always carried orchards of figs, mulberries, oranges, apricots, quince, walnuts, and pomegranates. Grain fields color the landscape green and gold.

Two facts are astonishing in this familiar story. First Jesus' willingness and ease in greeting a woman. First-century Judaism, the most masculine of the world's religions, allowed women no legal rights. A Jewish male thanked God daily that he was not born a woman and rabbis debated whether women had souls. Yet Jesus addressed a female stranger. No wonder she and the disciples were stunned!

In addition she was a Samaritan. Most Jews avoided Samaria, taking a roundabout route up the Jordan Valley, because they despised the Samaritans. Jesus seems to have had a gentle and open way of dealing with them and it may be that he "had to go" through Samaria, as John records, because he was determined to make himself known to this alienated people.

Samaria boasted a proud history. This was the home of the patriarch Jacob, the place of "Jacob's ladder." A white domed building nearby is said to contain the tomb of Joseph, Jacob's favored son.

When the Assyrians invaded in 721 B.C., Samaria was the most advanced region in Israel. Many Jewish inhabitants were taken captive and exiled. Some who remained married Assyrian immigrants. The resulting mixed-marriage families were ostracized by their southern neighbors, and branded "unclean," "impure." When the exiles returned, Samaritans were forbidden to take part in rebuilding the Temple or city walls in Jerusalem.

Cut off from their Jewish origins by virtual apartheid, they built their own temple, and created their own priesthood, consolidating the separation.

A small Samaritan sect remains in this area, though the population is predominantly Arab. Unfortunately, Nablus is a center of tension between Palestinians and Jews.

Pilgrims still visit Jacob's well on the West Bank. The well is 90 feet (28 m) deep. Visitors like to toss a rock in and count the four seconds it takes to create a splash at the bottom. There the springs that feed it still leap and bubble like the living water of which Jesus spoke.

God of all life, refresh our minds with the beauty of the land around us and with faith in Christ's gift of life flowing full and free.

Hebron

*Then Jacob charged them saying. "Bury me
with my ancestors . . . in the cave in the field
at Machpelah, near Mamre . . ."*

READ GENESIS 23:1–12, 25:8–10, 35:27–29, 49:29–32

Hebron is mentioned early in the history of the Judeo-Christian faith and it creates headlines in the daily news four thousand years later!

In the hilly country not far south of Bethlehem, Hebron nestles among vineyards and olive orchards. Its serene look belies the violence it has survived. Agriculture and light industry, pottery and glassworks, and a busy bazaar give Hebron the look of an average West Bank city, but it took center stage in world news when Israeli settlers were massacred in 1929 and in 1980, and again when in 1994 an enraged Jewish settler mowed down twenty-one Muslim worshipers in the mosque built over the Tomb of the Patriarchs.

It is the Tomb that draws Jewish, Christian, and Muslim pilgrims. Abraham is recognized as the Father of the Faith for the three great monotheistic world religions. Abraham purchased a burial ground here when Sarah died. Threading the book of Genesis are elaborately detailed stories of the deaths and burials in Hebron of Abraham and Sarah, Isaac and Rebecca, Jacob and Leah. (Jacob's favored wife Rachel is buried just outside Bethlehem. One guide says wryly, "Leah got him in the end!")

Many Christians are unaware that the familiar story of Abraham's willingness to sacrifice Isaac is retold in the Koran as the near-sacrifice of Ishmael, his first born and progenitor of the Arab people. It is this ancient rivalry that contributes to the tension, making this city the focus of international news.

Herod the Great, master builder in Israel, erected a magnificent temple over the cave where the founding families were buried. The massive foundation stones still stand. A Roman church, an early Arab mosque, a crusader church, an Egyptian Mamaluke mosque succeed one another, each built on Herod's foundation. From 1267 until the declaration of the State of Israel in 1967, Jews were forbidden to visit the tomb.

Christians trace the origins of their faith to Abraham. If a visit to Hebron is possible, it is an opportunity for the pilgrim to reflect on the one who four thousand years ago declared that there is but one God. That God is willing to communicate and relate to his creation, especially the human race, made in God's image.

God of Abraham and Sarah, Isaac and Rebecca, God of Jacob and Leah and Rachel, we stand in a long line of men and women who find meaning for life in the knowledge that you have made us for yourself, that you care and that you speak if we but listen. We are grateful for the faith and the faithful.

Jericho

Today salvation has come to this house.

READING: LUKE 19:1–10, MARK 10:46–52

More than 800 feet below sea level and watered by clear, bubbling springs, the oasis city of Jericho is rich in crops and green date palms. The splash of green on the Jordan Valley floor is etched against a background of windblown and sun-baked wasteland. Its sweet fragrance can be smelled across the dry plains. Roadside fruit stands offer refreshment after the dusty drive from Jerusalem or from the desolation of the Golan Heights and the war-torn borderland to the north. Jericho is one of the earliest cities in the world. In the excavations at the edge of the town are guard-towers that are probably the oldest structures on the face of the earth, dating back to 6000 B.C. In these digs are the stones of the city walls that tumbled as Joshua "fit the battle of Jericho."

In contrast to Jericho, precipitous steeps, craggy, bleak and dry, surround the pleasant oasis. This is the "Judean wilderness" into which Jesus retreated after his baptism in the nearby Jordan. It is a badland of rock, grit, and gravel, stark and sun-scorched. The contrast is stunning—from green to gray-brown, from verdant to desert, from grass to dust.

The two familiar Jericho stories carry something of the same sharp contrast. Zacchaeus, a selfish, detested tax-collector becomes a benefactor of the poor. Bartimaeus, born blind, pitiful and pleading, is born into a new world of sight and sunlight.

Gnarled, gray-green, sycamore trees still stand on Jericho streets, and the inhabitants will point out the one fabled to be the ancestor of the tree that Zacchaeus climbed to see Jesus pass by on his way to Jerusalem. Selfishness and greed marked the office of tax-collector in Jesus' day. They were seen as traitors, victimizing their own people for personal gain. Yet Jesus saw the possibility in the dry, parched spirit of Zacchaeus. His compassion, like the flumes that carried the water from Elisha's spring to irrigate the crops of Jericho, brought new life and growth to Zacchaeus.

Jesus was on his way to his death in Jerusalem when these events occurred. Jericho held powerful memories for him. Did he perhaps glance up from that Jericho street to the stony heights where today one can see the astonishing Monastery of the Temptation clinging to the nearly vertical cliffside? Did he draw fresh strength from the memory of his baptism nearby and the assurance that he was "the beloved one"?

Lord God, our lives are dry and parched without your presence, refreshing and renewing us daily. We pray that this time in this place may be blessed by your life-giving presence.

Qumran

Go now and write it before them on a tablet, and inscribe it in a book, so that it may be for the time to come as a witness forever.

READ: PSALM 119:1–8, 33–40

"The past is prologue to the future." Shakespeare's words are emblazoned above the entry to the Smithsonian Institute in Washington, D.C. He would have been stunned by both the depth of the past, as revealed in archaeology in the Holy Land, and by the speed of the future, symbolized in how accessible the Holy Land is to today's traveler.

Qumran in the Judean desert represents a startling fulfillment of Shakespeare's words. Here, in 1947, Bedouin goat herders discovered the Dead Sea scrolls in desolate caves near the Dead Sea. Past and future flowed together in a frenzy of excitement.

The scrolls had been rolled, stored in clay jars and hidden in the wilderness caves by scribes who feared annihilation by Roman legionnaires in 70 A.D. Almost certainly the Essenes, a Jewish sect who lived in monastic solitude in the Qumran desert location for almost two hundred years before the birth of Christ, were the scribes who copied the manuscripts. Among the many artifacts the archaeological teams discovered was a scriptorium, with desks and dried ink. Modern technology determined the dried ink and the ink on the scrolls were the same!

An elaborate baptistry and aqueduct system provided evidence that these holy men not only took the prescribed care when writing the divine names, that is, pronouncing the formula, "I intend to the write the Holy Name," they also washed or baptized themselves each time they wrote the sacred words.

Discovery of manuscripts from every Old Testament book except Esther rocked Judaism and Christianity. The texts were one thousand years older than any available at the time of the discovery, yet variations were few and insignificant! Such had been the reverence for the word!

Judaism and Christianity are religions of the book, as is Islam. Devotion to ensuring that "the book" is available to all, as close as possible to its original form, is an infinitely valuable dimension of Judeo-Christian history. Men and women have lived and died devoted to the message that has come in the scriptures and to the scriptures that contain the message. The Essenes were determined that the word would be preserved. Two thousand years later we are the heirs of their devotion. The excavations at Qumran are their memorial.

God who from the beginning came as the Word, we are awed that the word has found us, touched us, shaped our lives. We give thanks for the capacity to read, to absorb, to share, and to discuss. We are grateful to those so loyal to the word that they risked life to have it come to us in purity and power.

Masada

*Let us now praise famous ones and
our parents who begat us.
(Adapted from Ecclesiasticus in the Apocrypha.)*

READ: PSALM 150 FOUND IN PARCHMENT ON MASADA

"Masada shall not fall again!" For many years this was the shout of young recruits in the Israeli army as they completed graduation ceremonies held on the rock features of Masada 1,300 feet (400 m) above the Dead Sea. Masada stands as a symbol of Jewish defiance against all foes.

Its story is one of the most dramatic in military history. About fifty years after Christ's death the occupying Roman army had crushed all opposition in the Holy Land—with one exception. A powerful group of insurgents had destroyed the Roman garrison at Masada, taken over the mountain-top fortification with its vast cisterns of fresh water and storehouses holding enough food for ten years, and were harassing the Romans camped in the merciless desert beneath.

In 72 A.D. the Roman governor Flavius Silva determined to destroy the rebels. He marched at the head of the famous Tenth Legion and laid siege to the rock with ten thousand troops. After months of frustration Silva dismantled the old Herodian aqueduct and began to build on it a ramp that would carry his army up to the walls of the fortress.

For a time the Jewish forces prevented the project by rolling huge boulders down onto the builders, but when Silva began to use Jewish prisoners, their countrymen refused to continue the defense. The time came when it was clear that the Roman battering rams would breach the walls.

On the eve of the final assault the Jewish leader Eleazar Ben Yair faced the 967 inhabitants of Masada and gave them the alternatives—surrender or frustrate the Romans in a final act of defiance. He concluded, "Let our wives die undishonored and our children without knowing slavery; and when they are gone, let us do each other an ungrudging kindness, preserving our liberty as a whole funeral monument."[4] The next morning when the Romans broke through the wall they met only silence. They saw the bodies of 960 Jews, dead by their own hands. Only two women and five children survived to tell the story.

Stark, barren, the steep rock walls rise from the Judean desert, a monument to courage and commitment. If vigor permits, the pilgrim can bypass the cable car and climb the narrow twisting trail up the sheer sides of Masada, look down on the clear lines of the Roman encampments at the base, and feel for a moment what it must have been to join that proud party of patriots.

Lord God of the ages, our hearts and wills are stirred by the courage of those who have gone before us and have blazed a trail of valor and devotion. May our own weak wills be lifted to resist evil, to seek justice, and to love mercy, through Christ our Lord.

Be'er-Sheva

*Abraham planted a tamarisk tree in Be'er-Sheva,
and called there on the name of the Lord.*

READ: GENESIS 21:25–34

The Negev, Israel's southern desert, familiar from
news headlines, is also the setting for the stories of
Abraham and Isaac, Rebecca, Hagar and Ishmael.
The pilgrim traveling through the desert heat in air-
conditioned comfort wonders who would think of
this five thousand square miles of bleak and arid
waste as "The Promised Land."

Abraham's family was nomadic. They moved with
their flocks as the Bedouins do today. The one point
of return was Be'er-Sheva where Abraham purchased
a well to sustain his people in the dreadful heat. In
World War I Australian and New Zealand forces fighting in the Negev sang a powerful ballad, "The Wells
of Beer-Sheba," that told of their driving need for water. The waters of Be'er-Sheva have shaped the history of the Negev.

In no other part of the world is the desert being
thrust back so boisterously. Be'er-Sheva stands as a
symbol of the promise that the desert shall blossom
as the rose. A small courtyard built around Abraham's
well blooms scarlet with pomegranates, the national

flower. The air is fragrant with jasmine, oleander, bougainvillea, and hibiscus. The soil is fertile and needs only irrigation to supplement the meager rainfall. The pilgrim is reminded of Moses' promise to his people of, "a good land . . . of wheat and barley, of vines and fig trees." The huge, under-canvas Bedouin market held each Thursday brings together nomads and settlers, despite the tensions that still divide them.

Israelis recall their desert heritage. After a violent sandstorm had blown grit into every home in Jerusalem, a homemaker said, "It is good that we have sand in our luxurious homes. It reminds us of our ancestors wandering in the Negev that we might live in comfort."

In the earliest years of the new state Prime Minister Ben Gurion, touring south of Be'er-Sheva, came on a fledgling settlement, Sede Boker, where pioneers were creating homes in the wilderness. Moved by their courage he said, "Can I join you?" Shortly afterward he retired and did join them. One of his first questions was, "Why have you not planted trees?" They replied, "The experts tell us no trees can grow here." Ben Gurion's reply captures the nation's spirit of adventure. "There are only experts of the past: there are no experts of the future!"

God of all refreshment and renewal, come to our lives like rivers of water to a parched land. As we face the work that life requires grant us relief from the dry times that make life brittle. Gives us fresh strength, newborn hope, and a clear vision of your will.

Mount Sinai

. . . after the Israelites had gone out of the land of Egypt . . . they came into the wilderness of Sinai.

READ: EXODUS 19:1–9, 16–25, 20:1–17

The Judean desert is not just sandy dunes as one might suppose. It is rocky, rugged, chaotic. Serrated peaks bite at the sky. Strange, wind-sculpted rock formations glower like gargoyles. Rocky plateaus are scarred by the wadis (gullies) that carry off quick but heavy torrents in the brief rainy season. It is in this ominous, mysterious land, that monotheism came to birth.

Here that astonishing leader Moses changed the course of human history as he encountered the living God on a mountain top shrouded in mystery.

It is not as if the Sinai were unknown before Moses. It had long been a route joining Africa and the nations of the eastern Mediterranean. Nabatean camel caravans carried incense, silk, spices, and other luxuries. Others mined its mountains, and some fed their flocks on the scanty but resilient pastureland to be found in the steep valleys between naked desert peaks. Today over half of Israel is desert. Israelis have learned to live with this inhospitable terrain so successfully that their "experts" in desert living are recognized worldwide and are in demand in Africa and other desert lands.

But it is the intriguing story of Moses on Mount Horeb that draws the pilgrim to this raw and bone-dry land. Empress Helena, the relentless researcher of holy sites, established a monastery on what she believed was the site of "the burning bush," at the foot of Mount Sinai. It was later enlarged and fortified. In the nineteenth century the czars of Russia took a particular interest in the site and have left their mark on its decor. Fifteen hundred years after its founding the monastery still welcomes pilgrims. One can stay at a hostel in the monastery itself. Like most of the desert monasteries the number of residents is dwindling. At one time there were four hundred monks, now there is only a handful.

Its library contains ancient manuscripts second only to the Vatican in value. The Slav influence is evident in its vast collection of icons. The Church includes the fascinating Chapel of the Burning Bush, where the pilgrim must remove shoes as Moses did in approaching the bush. Those who are very fit can make the ascent in two to four hours to visit a small chapel and enjoy a breathtaking view.

One is awed by standing on the very ground that 3,500 years ago was the cradle of faith in one God.

Almighty, Creator, Loving God, we stand in awe before the remembrance of those who have encountered you in the wilderness. May we continue to learn and grow through the faith that they have passed on.

Bethlehem

Let us go over to Bethlehem and see . . .

READ: MATTHEW 2:1–12

Long have we blindly groped our stumbling road,
Seeking the light, though wandering oft astray,
But now the path shall be made plain to God—
He comes to show the way:
Long hath our journey been from lands afar,
Costly and splendid are the gifts we bring.
Tell us, we pray thee now, where lies the King,
For we have seen his star?

Lucy Maude Montgomery

Magi followed a star to Bethlehem. Christians still follow the star!

For sixteen centuries the Church of the Nativity has marked Christ's birthplace. It is the oldest church in the Holy Land, probably in the world.

Visitors approach the cruciform basilica across a walled cobblestone square and stoop to enter the four-foot, sixteenth-century "Door of Humility" (stoned in to prevent access to marauding horsemen). Close by, restored mosaics depict the wise men in ancient Persian costume. It is said that in 614, when the Persians were destroying all churches and convents, this one was spared because the invaders saw their likeness in the mosaic.

Several steps lead down to a marble-covered grotto, the traditional birthplace. Pilgrims kneel to touch the fourteen-point silver star set over the manger, fourteen points for the fourteen generations from Abraham to Jesus. A Latin text reads, "Here Christ was born."

The holy site is shared, decorated, and maintained by Roman Catholic, Greek Orthodox, and Armenian Christians. Their three concepts of beautification have created an eclectic mix of decor. Varied worship practices introduce incense, candles, clerical vestments, and liturgical forms of various sorts. Moreover, the visitor is surrounded by worshipers who experience high emotional devotion in a variety of ways. The visit can be overwhelming!

The Arab community in Bethlehem, often hostile to the Jewish presence, offers hospitality to guests from every nation. At Christmas thousands fill Manger Square with a festival of song and joy. Because not all Christians mark the same natal day, celebrations continue around denominational calendars.

In Arab-owned shops olive wood crèches are sought-after souvenirs. Christian Arabs (about 20 percent of Bethlehem's population) feel isolated in the State of Israel. In an ecumenical spirit, they request the prayers of pilgrims, especially on Christmas Eve.

God of gold, we seek your glory:
the richness that transforms drabness into color,
God of incense, we offer you our spoken and
unspeakable longing.
God of myrrh, we cry out to you in our suffering and
our rage at continuing injustice.
We pray to you, God with us, Emmanuel.
          (*Voices United* 88, adapted and abridged)

Shepherds' Field

In that region were shepherds living in the fields,
keeping watch over their flocks . . .

READ: PSALM 23, 1 SAMUEL 16:1–13, LUKE 2:8–20,
JOHN 10:14–16

The hills of the Holy Land are pasture land for sheep
as they have been since ancient times.

The pilgrim encounters sheep on the barbed wire
borderland between Israel and its hostile neighbors,
where shepherds are trained in surveillance for border infiltration. Sheep are herded in the seemingly
desolate rocky ledges of the Judean wilderness where
only the hardiest vegetation survives the scorching
sun. Sheep bumble along through village streets in
trusting obedience to the guidance of their shepherds.

This common part of life in the Holy Land, sheep
and shepherds, is honored throughout the Bible.
Probably the best known passage in the Old Testament, "The LORD is my shepherd . . .," was composed
by David, a shepherd chosen to be king. The Lord is
a shepherd! Such a humble, yet gracious, metaphor!
On many occasions Jesus mentions sheep, abundant
on the hills of Galilee then as now.

Bethlehem is surrounded by gentle countryside
where sheep and goats are pastured. Two scenes of
Bethlehem fields stir the imagination as one leaves

the Church of the Nativity in Bethlehem to travel the short distance to Shepherds' Field.

One picture illustrates the Old Testament account in which the prophet Samuel is seeking a king for Israel. Seven of Jesse's sons are introduced but none is chosen of the Lord. Finally, as one senses Samuel's desperation, he sends for the youngest, David, who is tending the sheep. Samuel has the "Aha" of recognition and, to the amazement of all, on the spot anoints David, the young shepherd, King of Israel.

The second picture is from the night when Jesus was born. A divine message is given to shepherds keeping watch over their flocks near Bethlehem. Two sites are claimed for this event. In each instance the scene is believable. It is all there. It is just as one believed it was when donning the shepherd's costume for the Christmas pageant long ago.

In the Grotto of the Shepherds and in the pristine church, a gift of Canada, there is calm and peacefulness. Simple worship centers are used by those moved to praise God for the joyous news of Christ's birth. The shepherd symbol stayed with Jesus throughout his ministry. "I am the Good Shepherd, I know my own and my own know me." In him there is utter caring and knowledge of his earthly flock.

Great Shepherd of the Sheep, guiding, protecting God, we thank you for the centuries old assurance that you care for us as a guardian shepherd cares for the flock, and we are grateful.

Bethany

Six days before the Passover Jesus came to Bethany.

READ: JOHN 11:1–53

John records that Jesus stopped in Bethany just five days before his death. Only three miles from Jerusalem, over the Mount of Olives, this was the home of Lazarus, Mary, and Martha. It seems impossible that a community should maintain the same character and spirit over the centuries, yet travelers have found that small Arab town of El Azariah, old Bethany, to be especially warm and welcoming.

The traditional location of the home is questionable. There is, however, great value in designating a particular spot as a memorial whether or not it is geographically the very piece of ground on which that event took place. The site is made holy by the veneration and memories that centuries of pilgrims have brought to it.

Jesus' first recorded visit to Bethany provided the well-known conversations in the home of Martha and Mary. Here Jesus performed his most memorable miracle, the raising of their brother, Lazarus. In his last days he chose to sleep under his roof. In another home in Bethany, that of Simon the Leper, Mary anointed his feet with precious ointment and dried them with her hair.

The village stands on the eastern slope of the Mount of Olives, at the dividing line between the verdant hillside and the beginning of the dry, stony land that drops off to Jericho and the Dead Sea.

Churches have been built and destroyed at this place. A mosque built here in the sixteenth century remains. For a number of years Christians were unable to visit the tomb of Lazarus, until the Franciscans gained permission to create a twenty-four-step passageway to the cavernous grotto under the mosque where Lazarus may have lain.

Life for most of the inhabitants of Bethany is simple. In a courtyard near the tomb Arab women wash laundry by hand and carefully use and reuse precious water. Though they are separated from tourists by language, religion, and culture, the women welcome courtyard conversation. Many pilgrims take home clay lamps as souvenirs, symbols of a town known for its hospitality to Jesus.

On the outside wall of the home is a plaque that reads in part, "Today, as in the past, the love of Jesus seeks a refuge where he is lovingly expected and where he can rest. He longs for us to empty our hearts and lovingly receive him."

God of the universe, Creator of our orbiting planet, our hearts are warmed by words of friendship and hospitality. We are grateful for the little household of Bethany that reminds us that the deepest fellowship can reach across all dividing lines, even the chasm between this world and the next.

Jerusalem

Pray for the peace of Jerusalem.

READ: PSALMS 87, 122, 125, 128, LUKE 19:41–44

Three familiar phrases describe Jerusalem. "Let us go up to Jerusalem." Set on a commanding height of land that sprawls across a spine of limestone hills, David's choice for the capital city, Jerusalem is powerfully located for defense, for trade, and for beauty. The ancients referred to Jerusalem as the "navel of the world."

Many of the familiar Psalms were written for pilgrims of the Jewish faith journeying to Jerusalem. They approached the city from lower ground, coming up to Jerusalem and the accepted way was to come singing. The modern pilgrim is as moved by the first sight of the walls of Jerusalem as those footsore pilgrims were.

"Jerusalem the golden!" The city is golden due to an ordinance that requires buildings to be constructed of honey-colored limestone that is quarried nearby. In the dawnlight or in the slanting beams of the setting sun, the city glows like the finest gold.

"The Holy City." Jerusalem also glows with the aura of a city with a secret, an open secret. This is the home of faith. Abraham Heschel said, "In order to see Jerusalem you must hear it."[5] At the Western Wall the pilgrim can hear above the quiet swaying chant of Kedushah, the high pitched call of the muezzin, bidding Muslims to prayer, and, in the background, the boom of bells from the Church of the Holy Sepulchre. This seems sometimes competitive, sometimes harmonious.

The city is redolent with the past, yet its holiness is not tied to history. The saga of God touching human life comes alive in this place for those who come as witnesses, not just onlookers; as pilgrims, not just tourists. To walk into Jerusalem is to walk into a dream, into a prayer. Teddy Kollek, well-known former mayor, used to tell visitors, "From here a phone call 'upstairs' is not long distance."

At the same time it is a most cosmopolitan, polyglot city in which a key descriptive word is "multiplicity." Jerusalem is immediately multiple. Old and new, east and west, are juxtaposed in its buildings, its peoples, its sounds, smells, and sights. Laden donkeys obstruct Mercedes on busy city thoroughfares. Heavily veiled women carrying home groceries in plastic pails balanced on their heads, walk beside svelte businesswomen. The costumes of eighteenth-century mid-European shtetls are standard dress for many.

One writer describes the city as "a cradle of hope where the final clash of civilization seems always at hand."[6] Let us pray for the peace of Jerusalem.

Brooding God, may the prayers for peace that rise across the face of our planet come to you and in your power and love, answer.

Mount of Olives

He came out and went, as was his custom,
to the Mount of Olives.

READ: MATTHEW 21:1–17

Jerusalem is a city set among low mountains. To the east is the beautiful Mount of Olives, or Olivet, named for the abundance of luxuriant olive trees. Jesus, with his disciples, spent time in this serene and safe place, near Jerusalem, yet away from its intrigues. Many of the recorded events of Jesus' life are commemorated here with churches on traditional holy sites. No Holy Land place offers more opportunity to recollect and reflect on the life and Passion of our Lord.

After arriving by bus, visitors descend the Mount of Olives on foot with travelers from around the world, aware that they also join company with Christians through the centuries.

The Chapel of the Ascension atop the Mount marks the rock from which tradition claims Jesus ascended to heaven. Peddlers offer olive wood souvenirs and postcards, and camel owners insist that you'd be better riding down the Mount. You focus on the incredible historic view across the Kidron Valley to Jerusalem the Golden, and continue your pilgrimage. This is a very special walk! Pilgrims are moved to sing, pray, or conduct services of worship. Passers-by are usually welcome to participate.

The Church of the Pater Noster, on the traditional site of the gift of the Lord's Prayer, features sixty-two tiled mosaic panels with the Lord's Prayer glazed in a different language on each one. The panels, inset in the cloister walls, invite reflection.

The Church of Our Lord's Tears, Dominus Flavit, commemorates in stunning, tear-shaped architecture the moment on Palm Sunday when Jesus stopped the triumphal procession and wept over Jerusalem. Wrought iron latticework above the altar frames a view of the Holy City.

The Church of All Nations at the foot of the Mount of Olives is erected over the place made holy by the prayers and agony of Jesus. Contributions by sixteen countries led to its completion in 1924, and are acknowledged by the countries' coats of arms in the beautifully decorated cupola. Windows of translucent bluish-purple alabaster create a subdued atmosphere. This church, and the seven-spired, golden-domed church of Mary Magdalene are near the Garden of Gethsemane.

Over by the wall a donkey stands untethered and alone, making real Jesus' strange directive, "You will find an ass untied and a colt . . . bring them to me."

This day the pilgrim surely walks where Jesus walked!

God of the ages, thank you for this journey
backwards in time. In our hearts, we join in the glad
hosannas of this hillside and are grateful.

Olive Trees

The LORD your God is bringing you into a good land
. . a land of fig trees and pomegranates, a land of
olive trees and honey . . .

READ: DEUTERONOMY 8:1–10, 24:19–22,
ROMANS 11:17–24

The Mount of Olives, outside Jerusalem, is the site of many events recorded in the Bible. We know the happenings but seldom think about the olive trees that give the mountain its name. Olive trees have been a life-giving resource in the Holy Land since before the time of Christ. Olive trees are well suited to the climate of Israel as they like dry, limestone soil and will often flourish where other trees will not take root. Olive trees have been especially important to the poor. The olives, the shade, the wood, and the oil for cooking, for medicinal purposes, and for light have long given sustenance to the people of this land.

In the Garden of Gethsemane (the word means "olive press") there are eight gray, gnarled olive trees whose age is lost in antiquity. Some botonists believe they may be over three thousand years old. If they were not in the garden when Jesus prayed in his night of agony, they are the offspring of those very trees.

Israeli law forbids the cutting of olive trees. To protect property from expropriation Israeli farmers often include olive trees in their plantings so their property is likely to remain untouchable.

Trees of any kind are precious in the Holy Land. In an extensive program of reforestation sixty million trees have been planted. In rabbinical tradition, when the Messiah gathers his people one may not say, "I must finish my prayers," but may say, "I must first plant this tree."

Carved olive wood crèches, crosses, statues, found principally in Bethlehem, are popular souvenirs. Small olive wood cups are often used by pilgrims for celebration of the Lord's Supper in the Holy Land. They can be purchased reasonably to present to congregations back home. Using them for communion on their return symbolizes the deep bond between their land and the Holy Land that provides the cup and that engendered the ritual meal.

In Romans, Paul describes the Christian as a wild olive branch grafted into the root, God's love. God grafts us to his tree of life in order that we may grow and receive nurturance there. Sophisticated author Paul knew he and his readers could learn from this metaphor of a common object—the olive tree!

God of Creation, these reminders of an age long past stand, gnarled, twisted, battered by wind and weather. As Jesus found strength for his trial among these ancient trees so may we draw from his example strength for struggles of our own.

St. Anne's Church

Hear my son, . . . reject not your mother's teaching.

READ: PROVERBS 31:10–31, LUKE 1:46–56

In the acoustically perfect Church of St. Anne, located a few yards from St. Stephen's Gate, pilgrim choirs arrive with music in hand to praise God in whatever is their native tongue. This church, built in 1142 by Avda, the widow of Baldwin, the crusader king, is simple in comparison with many structures that mark the holy sites.

Tradition has Joachim and Anne, the parents of Mary, living in Jerusalem at the time of Mary's birth. The church was erected to commemorate their presence and it has about it a gentle welcoming atmosphere. On the front of the altar the art depicts the Annunciation, the Nativity, and the Descent from the cross. On one side Mary is being taught by her mother. On the other is her presentation in the temple.

At the back of the church is a marble statue of the mother, Anne, with her arm encircling a preteen Mary. Candles burn at the base of the statue and flowers soften the gray tones of the stone church.

In spring and early summer, flowers bloom in profusion in the garden surrounding the church and the song of birds is a prelude to the music being sung, almost continuously, in the sanctuary.

There are several legends about Mary's birthplace, but this one place invites reflection on the grandmother of Christ.

How would she respond to the Annunication news?

Did she know of the flight into Egypt?

Was she present when her grandson caused a sensation by curing a lame man in the waters of the pool of Bethesda a stone's throw from her home?

Could she hear the cheering at the triumphal entry into Jerusalem?

Where was she when Jesus appeared before Pilate?

Could she hear the shouts of "Crucify him!" from the Antonium close by?

We can be sure that the mother of Mary was an exemplary mother to have nurtured the young woman chosen of God for greatness. Somewhere, perhaps close at hand in Jerusalem, she was there to share some of the mystery that Mary carried in her heart.

Loving God, we are grateful for the women we meet in your Holy Word. We are learning so much about them in this land where they lived, married, had children, served husbands, and, like us, worshiped you, O LORD. Stir our imaginations that we may more clearly understand our faith heritage.

The Via Dolorosa

The son must undergo great suffering
. . . and be killed.

READ: LUKE 23:26–49

There is a theme of scriptural "fulfillment" in the events of Good Friday, as in much of Jesus' ministry. It was the freedom festival, Passover, the time when, in Jewish tradition, a lamb was killed at 12 noon and eaten at 3:00 P.M. Jesus became the Pascal Lamb, sacrificing himself for the sin of the world. He walked the Way of Sorrows to be nailed to a cross at noon and to die by midafternoon.

Pilgrims follow his walk from the Praetorium, the Roman judgment hall, through the crowded walkways of old Jerusalem. Each week priests ceremoniously carry a wooden cross along the Via Dolorosa, but visitors follow the ceramic signs and numbers marking the Stations of the Cross any time.

The Protestant asks: "What are the Stations of the Cross?" They are markers that evoke a memory of the tragic death processional. Roman Catholic churches have for centuries incorporated the Stations into their sanctuaries to ritualize this walk and to prompt meditation on the Way of Sorrows.

The Jerusalem crowds and the shoppers in the souks are not conducive to pilgrim meditation but these narrow cobblestone passages would surely have been as bustling and confusing for Christ's walk.

The convent of the Sisters of Zion, early on the walk, offers pilgrims sanctuary and an explanatory model of the walk. Below the convent floor one can actually walk on the pavement of the Antonia Fortress and view the limestone lithostrotos, the floor on which the Roman soldiers scratched out their gambling game.

The last five Stations are in the Church of the Holy Sepulchre. From the newly refurbished sun-ray dome to the heavily ornamented tomb where Jesus' body is said to have lain, the custodians—Roman Catholic, Armenian, Greek and Syrian Orthodox, Ethiopian and Egyptian Copt—have each embellished the tomb of Christ with exquisite decor according to their own traditions.

To get centered in this complex of shrines, relics, and chapels is not easy. Continuing the Stations, pilgrims mount a staircase that leads to the summit of the sixteen-foot rock reputed to be Calvary. In the "Nailing to the Cross" chapels pilgrims move through the remaining Stations.

The range of emotions experienced in this amazing sanctuary can be overwhelming, but need not prevent the visitor from observing and participating. Even the simple act of prayerfully lighting a candle and placing the holder in "the sands of time" can create a sense of completion. "It is finished."

In this overwhelming place, O God grant quiet assurance of the presence of the risen Christ.

*T*he Garden Tomb

*On the first day of the week Mary Magdalene
came to the tomb early.*

READ: JOHN 20:1–18

"Sir, if you have carried him away, tell me where you have laid him . . ."

Since Mary Magdalene's first plaintive query to the would-be gardener, believers have searched for the tomb of the risen Lord. At his birth there was the question, "Where is he that is born King of the Jews, that we may worship him?" At his death there was the question, "Where is he?" There is an earthly longing to participate in the divine presence of Christ.

The quest for the burial place continued over time with holy passion, debate, and disagreement. Would it be inside the walls of Jerusalem? Where were the walls in Jesus time? Controversy, even war, raged over the sepulchre.

Jesus was buried near Calvary, the place of crucifixion. All four evangelists record that Joseph of Arimathea, a wealthy man, offered to have Jesus buried in his own rock-hewn tomb, close to the place of crucifixion. The Gospels describe the burial place at Golgotha, as a skull-shaped knoll outside the walls, near the Damascus Gate close to the city and near a well-used thoroughfare. Two locations are now venerated as the tomb. Each is visited by Holy Land pilgrims.

The Church of the Holy Sepulchre stands where a church was erected by Empress Helena, great benefactress of Christianity, to commemorate the burial place. The present huge edifice was enlarged by the crusaders and has had many changes and aggrandizements over time.

A tomb that fit the biblical description outside the present north wall was first suggested in the mid-nineteenth century and it rapidly became favored by Protestants as a probable site. In 1882, General C. E. Gordon, who fell in battle at Khartoum in 1885, promoted the acceptance of this location in Palestine and in his native England. A foundation to acquire, develop, and care for this second location was established in England. Gordon died certain that he had accurately located the Garden Tomb. "Gordon's Calvary" is maintained and hosted by the volunteer organization he started.

Visitors to the Garden Tomb are guided through rock gardens to the tomb and then to seats for meditation and, if desired, for holy communion. Birds singing, pilgrims singing, and the rugged beauty of the location are conducive to reflection and renewal.

The tranquillity and beauty are not marred by the noise of the bustling city nor the uproar from the nearby bus depot. One does recall another ancient question. "Why seek ye the living among the dead?"

"He lives!"

God of earth and heaven, having been blessed by this pilgrimage, what is your will for me?

*T*he Western Wall

The house that King Solomon built for the LORD . . .

READ: 1 KINGS 6:1–14

The pilgrim comes to a most familiar scene—the
Western Wall, the Wailing Wall. Here elderly Jews,
prayer shawls across their shoulders, alongside
young soldiers with uzis on theirs, recite their
prayers with the little hopping movement that tells
they have come to a holy word. There may be a bar
mitzvah at the wall, perhaps involving North African
Jews whose families will dance, whistle, and throw
candy in exuberance.

Countless notes are tucked into every crack and
crevice in the stone wall. Tiny letters to God are a way
of conveying deepest longing on this sacred ground.
Civic authorities regard this act solemnly, gathering
the notes regularly to reverently inter them in a special place.

Worshipers come rejoicing at having free access to
the Wall at any time, after centuries of either being
barred entirely or of having only rare days of access.

Why does this 52-foot (16 m) length of stone wall
command such reverence? For centuries it was the last
visible remnant of the mighty wall that surrounded
what is now known as the temple compound. Every

Jew knows how David, the hero-king, dreamt of building a temple fit for Adonai, but was denied. His son Solomon was the first builder, but Babylonians destroyed that Temple. Exiles returning from Babylon under Ezra rebuilt on a modest scale. It was Herod the Great who created an edifice that should have been the eighth wonder of the ancient world!

The State has put astonishing energy, vision, and funding into archaeology, excavating countless tons of earth to expose its grandeur. Recent excavation has revealed foundation stones that are the second largest found in the ancient world. Standing at the foot of those foundation stones and looking up the walls and along their length, one is stunned by the massive architecture.

For the devout Jew the Temple was a place of encounter with the living God. There the awesome mystery of Adonai who visited this chosen people was reenacted and renewed. Jesus was dedicated in the Temple. His family made a Temple pilgrimage when he was twelve. He drove the money changers out of the Temple in anger!

Its loss when the Romans destroyed it in 70 A.D. has been ritualized by Jewish practices ever since. It has a place even in the wedding ceremony as the glass is ground under the groom's foot, a reminder that Jews still mourn the loss of the Temple.

God of our fathers and mothers, may we remain true to the best of our heritage. We sense the rejoicing and the mourning of those who have bequeathed us our faith. We would draw strength from each.

Dome of the Rock

*I have built you an exalted house, a place
for you to dwell in forever.*

READ: GENESIS 22:2, KINGS 5:1–6, 6:1, 7:51, 8:22–30

The glow of the magnificent golden Dome of the
Rock and the serene elegance of the Persian blue tile
facade of its perfectly proportioned octagonal shrine,
dominates the Jerusalem skyline. Restored and embellished many times since it was erected, it became
even more splendid recently when King Hussein of
Jordan had the dome reconstructed with lighter material, then regilded with 80 kilos of 24 karat gold!

This Muslim monument was built in the seventh
century over the historical "Rock" of Mount Moriah.
The rock, 30 feet (10 m) long and 24 feet (8 m) wide,
occupies the center of the shrine and is surrounded
by lavish decor, stained glass windows, and pillars of
marble. Glass partitions keep souvenir hunters from
temptation! The rock is sacred to both Muslim and
Jew and is a significant symbol of faith for Christians.

Islamic tradition holds that Mohammed, in a vision,
ascended from the rock with the angel Gabriel on a
night journey to "The Far Distant Place of Worship,"
referred to in the holy writing of Islam, the Sura. Although Mohammed never traveled to Jerusalem, the
Rock became central to the Islamic faith.

In Jewish tradition it was on this rock on Mount Moriah that Abraham prepared to sacrifice his son, Isaac. Later King Solomon centered his magnificent temple on the Rock. The Temple was home for the Ark, a sacrificial altar, and a royal chapel. The holy of holies, built over the rock, was surrounded by a three-story rectangular outer wall covering several acres.

Access to the Dome of the Rock is allowed except during times of prayer.

The Al Aqsa Mosque (meaning, "the farthest place") with its silver-colored dome is a shrine that accommodates five thousand for prayer and is also part of the temple compound. As Muslim women join pilgrims in the circular promenade one understands the "modest dress" requirement. Bearded men, in loose cotton suits move slowly to Al Aqsa for prayer at the sound of the muezzin. Muslim devotion requires formal prayer, five times a day.

As the Christian stands amid the dazzling grandeur of the ancient shrine, observing unfamiliar, even mysterious, ways of worship, emotions run high.

It is said that in 638, when Caliph Omar, Arab conqueror of Jerusalem, visited the Church of the Holy Sepulchre, he deigned not to enter but simply knelt in prayer outside. Perhaps this is the gracious model for today's guests in Jerusalem.

God of all peoples, keep our minds and hearts open, that we may be given a larger vision of your way in the world, for you are God of all nations, all races, all people.

Mount Zion

Walk about Zion, go round about it
. . . go through its citadels.

READ: PSALM 48, LUKE 22:7–22

Jerusalem is a city of hills. Many remarkable places to visit are located on two hills just south of the present walls of the Old City. The easterly hill, Mount Ofel, marks the first Jerusalem, the City of David and of Solomon. On this hill is the Spring of Gehon. Ingenious engineering seven hundred years before Christ created a tunnel so the spring could feed the Pool of Siloam inside the city walls, allowing Jerusalem to withstand several sieges.

On its slope stands the lovely Barluzzi Church of St. Peter in Gallicantu (meaning "cock-crow"), reputedly built over the house of the high priest Caiphas. Here Peter made his fateful denial and here the pilgrim is bound to reflect on how easily betrayal comes, even to those most committed.

The other hill bears the celebrated name, Mount Zion. Several churches and Jewish centers of devotion are scattered across its flank. Cemeteries cover much of the hillside. Oscar Schindler is buried there.

The graceful Benedictine Church of the Dormition, outstanding landmark on the hill, is purported to be the last resting place of Mary, the mother of Christ, before, according to Roman Catholic belief, she was taken bodily into heaven. It has many beautiful features, mosaics, carved doors, sculptures, and sumptuously furnished chapels.

Nearby is the major point of interest for the Christian pilgrim, the room of the Last Supper. Although the exact location of the upper room is not known, there seems to be strong likelihood that the present room lies close to the original. A bold stone structure, it is not "painting perfect," but is hallowed by the feet of pilgrims who enter worshipfully to praise God and to commemorate Christ's last supper and the institution of Holy Communion.

Curiously, it was many years after the first Christian shrine was erected here that Jewish rabbinical scholars discovered what they believed to be the Tomb of David below. A visit to this tomb is a deep spiritual experience for religious Jews. After the Western Wall, it is Judaism's most sacred ground. The mammoth mausoleum is decorated with heavily embroidered royal purple fabric. On it is mounted a silver Torah crown for Israel's most illustrious leader and king.

God, we give you thanks for those who have cared to search and to research the lives of your servants and to commemorate them in wood and stone, marble, silver, and gold, and in art forms according to the traditions they know.

Shrine of the Book

*In the beginning was the Word
. . . and the Word was God.*

READ: DEUTERONOMY 6:1–9

Western pilgrims to Israel are startled by the indefatigability of generations of people driven by passionate belief in their religion and their national heritage who have built and rebuilt grand monuments, places of worship and assembly, obliterated by the sands of time. Still the indomitable will to refresh the human spirit with beauty and remembrance reappears in successive generations.

There are many ancient and many recent objects of beauty in Israel. A most unusual twentieth-century construction is the Shrine of the Book, honoring the memory of D. Samuel and Jeane H. Gottesman.

The Dead Sea scrolls, the oldest biblical manuscripts in existence, were discovered in earthen jars in caves of the desert area around Qumran. The parchments, written in clearly decipherable Hebrew, were purchased, scrutinized, and recognized as invaluable sacred relics. The Essenes, a reclusive, almost monastic, sect of scholarly Jews, many of whom chose to live in desert seclusion, were most surely the scribes who copied the scriptures. These are now housed in the Shrine of the Book in Jerusalem.

Mounting the steps to the Shrine the pilgrim encounters a high, black basalt wall alongside a modern white dome. The stark wall symbolizes the Children of Darkness, and the sparkling white dome, the Children of Light, dominant opposing themes in Essene literature and theology. The dome is in the shape of the lid that capped the earthen jars containing the scrolls.

The Shrine itself is an underground structure recalling the caves in which the scrolls were found. Atmospheric pressure, temperature, and humidity within the Shrine are regulated to preserve the treasures in conditions similar to the dry, hot climate of the Judean desert. The central feature is a facsimile of the Isaiah scroll stretched on a cylinder that permits a close-up view of the writing. Nearby a fragile fragment of an original leather scroll is mounted in a special display case.

It may surprise the pilgrim to hear a teenaged Jewish visitor from North America, a pack on her back, reading this two-thousand-year-old scroll as if it were a current newspaper article! The explanation is that Hebrew is written and spoken in Israel today as it was at the time of Jesus. Jews are the only people to have preserved their written and oral language so long despite separation, subjugation, and near annihilation!

God of all time, you have ensured the safe passage of truth from generation to generation. Grant that we may share our heritage with our descendants and honor those who have preserved the truth for us.

Yad Vashem

How long, O Lord? Will you forget me forever?

READ: PSALMS 3, 13

A visit to the Holocaust Museum at Yad Vashem is a shattering experience. How is it that a nation regarded as the most cultured on earth, with more university graduates per capita than any other nation, that led the world in music, literature, and science, could have slaughtered six million human beings in a stunningly merciless manner?

It is a question that haunts the literature of the century. Jewish theologians raise the question: Can there be belief in God after the Holocaust?

The Museum itself is organized to lead the visitor through the gradually accelerating madness that led to this tragedy. Most poignant are photos of children playing hopscotch waiting their turn at the gas chambers as guards look on. Within the Museum a disembodied voice pronounces the names of the victims as the visitor walks through a star-studded twilight pathway.

Yad Vashem is a monument to the tragic ambiguity in the human soul, a soul capable of sublime self-sacrifice for the sake of others and at the same time capable of unimaginable barbarism. The reproach of the Jewish people for all the inhuman acts of butchery that stain the pages of western history is embedded here. The pilgrim takes a fresh look at the doctrine of original sin!

Still it also remains a place of promise. One enters the Museum through a long avenue of trees, "The Avenue of the Just." Each tree honors a person or group who came to the aid of Jews during the dark time of the Holocaust.

The film *Schindler's List* tells of one who acted. Ironically, the ambiguous mixture of motives that resides in the human spirit is tragically evident in Oscar Schindler.

The Avenue represents many stories. For example, Princess Alice of Greece, mother of Prince Philip, hid a Jewish family in the grounds of the Royal Palace in Athens for thirteen months. In 1994 Prince Philip visited Yad Vashem to receive the Medal of Honor awarded posthumously to his mother, who, according to her dying wish, was buried at the Church of Mary Magdalene on the Mount of Olives. Many less famous names are gratefully remembered and commemorated. Over it all there is the powerful biblical assurance that God knows us each by name. A Psalm that expresses the age-old sorrow of the Jewish people begins "How long, O LORD? Will you forget me forever?" but ends, "But I trusted in your steadfast love; my heart shall rejoice in your salvation."

Out of the depths of all the pain in human history, we cry to you, O LORD, "How long?" Grant that the policies and practices of our nation may courageously act for peace and compassion, that your Kingdom may come, your will be done.

Jerusalem—The New City

Out of Zion, the perfection of beauty,
God shines forth.

READ: PSALMS 125, 126

Walking the streets of Jerusalem is like being "on stage" in an ongoing drama. The Old City draws the visitor, but the city that lies outside the walls offers much. For example, on the west side of the city, close to a cluster of popular hotels, a short stroll can commence at the elegant King David Hotel, Jerusalem's most prestigious. It entered the history books in 1946 when a wing, housing the British military headquarters, was blown up by a Jewish guerrilla group protesting the British occupation. Across the street the stately YMCA, like no other, is the work of the architect who designed the Empire State Building.

Close-by Liberty Bell Park contains a replica of the American bell presented by U.S. President L. B. Johnson. The gift brought back home the text that is inscribed on the rim of the bell, "Proclaim liberty throughout the land . . .," the words from Leviticus that were used to proclaim the State of Israel in 1948.

Just down the street is a notable landmark, a windmill! It contains a museum honoring the labors of the Sheriff of London, wealthy stockbroker Sir Moses Montefiore. He established the charming Yemen

Moshe residential area surrounding the mill. Montefiore, a quixotic character, came from his home in England fourteen times to encourage Jews to move from their crowded quarter in the Old City and take possession of land outside the walls. The windmill, used to grind wheat, was built to make the people self-sufficient. His last trip was in 1885 when he was nearly a hundred years old.

A short distance away is Wingate Square, commemorating a colorful English leader who arrived in the thirties to fight Arab rebels. He built his very successful battle strategy around biblical texts, especially from the story of Joshua.

Nearby is a Scottish church dedicated to Robert the Bruce who, in 1329 as he lay dying said, "When I was in danger I vowed to God to go and fight in the Holy Land. But though I know now my body cannot go hither, yet will I send my heart to fulfill my vow." Legend has it that his loyal followers attempted to carry out his wishes but the heart was lost while they were fighting their way through Spain.

Professor P. Peli of Jerusalem, puts it graciously, "Many hearts live in Jerusalem whose bodies have never come." The Christian whose loyalty to Jesus Christ has made so much of Jerusalem familiar will know what he means.

God of Zion, we are grateful for the countless stories that gather 'round this land. Even when tarnished with the frailties of human intention, they give us grounds for hope and examples of dedication.

Chagall Windows

These are the names of the sons of Israel . . .

READ: GENESIS 49:1–28, DEUTERONOMY 33

A pleasant day trip from Jerusalem takes the pilgrim through terraced slopes and vineyards to the garden suburb of Ein Kerem, the "city in Judea," the home of Elizabeth.

In Ein Kerem, the traditional birthplace of John the Baptist and the town to which Mary journeyed to visit her cousin, is the Church of the Visitation. It is the work of architect Barluzzi whose elegant artistry is evident in many Holy Land churches, especially the Church of the Beatitudes in Galilee. A modern fresco depicting the encounter of Mary and Elizabeth forms the church's facade.

One climbs to the heights above Ein Kerem for a visit to the Hadassah Medical Center, Ein Kerem. The Hadassah women's movement is named for the myrtle tree, symbol of honor and praise. Its members are committed to Zionism and act to improve the quality of life for Jewish people by promoting health, joy, beauty, and purpose.

The pilgrim walks through the heart of the hospital to reach the synagogue/chapel. In it is a stunning, swirling, riot of color, shape, and symbolism. These are the twelve stained glass windows by Marc Chagall that depict the twelve tribes of Israel.

It is instructive, and rather fun, for the pilgrim to read the two passages cited above and then to try to match the windows to the impressions of the twelve tribes, as described by Jacob and Moses. A feeling for the geography of the areas assigned each tribe helps. Birds, snakes, and mythical creatures, arks, menorahs, pottery, all symbols from Jewish history, float in vibrant stained glass, each color representing one of the gems in the breastplate of the High Priest. In an interview Chagall said, "It came to me as easily as song to a bird."

At the dedication, he said "All the time I was working I felt my father and my mother were looking over my shoulder, and behind them were Jews, millions of other vanished Jews of yesterday and a thousand years ago." This vision enlivens the windows with a superb blending of past and present. The present became real when, during the Six Day War in 1967, shells smashed some of the windows. Chagall wired from France, "You take care of the war. I'll take care of the windows." He left one bullet hole as a reminder of the contemporary significance of history.

God of history, we gather fresh strength from the example of those who have found renewal in the challenges of conflict and distress. We thank you for the artists who have enriched our lives with beauty, grace, and panache.

ISRAEL

LEBANON

• Caesarea Philippi

Mediterranean Sea

• Akko
• Safed

Capernaum •

SYRIA

• Haifa
Tiberias •
Sea of Galilee
Sepphoris •
• Cana
Carmel •
Nazareth

Caesarea
Megiddo
Jordan River

Hadera •

• Nablus

Tel-Aviv Yafo
Joppa

Jericho •

Jerusalem ⊕ Bethany
Qumran •

Bethlehem •
JORDAN

• Hebron

Masada •
Dead Sea
Be'er-Sheva

EGYPT

JERUSALEM

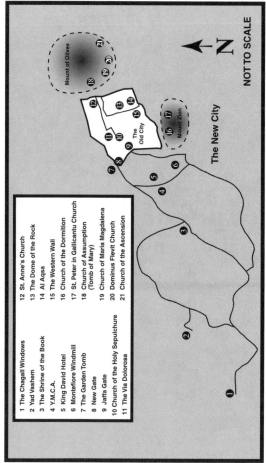

1 The Chagall Windows
2 Yad Vashem
3 The Shrine of the Book
4 Y.M.C.A.
5 King David Hotel
6 Montefiore Windmill
7 The Garden Tomb
8 New Gate
9 Jaffa Gate
10 Church of the Holy Sepulchre
11 The Via Dolorosa

12 St. Anne's Church
13 The Dome of the Rock
14 Al Aqsa
15 The Western Wall
16 Church of the Dormition
17 St. Peter in Gallicantu Church
18 Church of Assumption (Tomb of Mary)
19 Church of Maria Magdalena
20 Dominus Flevit Church
21 Church of the Ascension

The New City

The Old City

Mount of Olives

Mount Zion

N

NOT TO SCALE

*P*salms

Psalm 121 A Song of Ascents.

I lift up my eyes to the hills—
*   where does my help come from?*
My help comes from the LORD,
*   the Maker of heaven and earth.*
He will not let your foot slip—
*   he who watches over you will not slumber;*
indeed, he who watches over Israel
*   will neither slumber nor sleep.*
The LORD watches over you—
*   the LORD is your shade at your right hand;*
the sun will not harm you by day,
*   nor the moon by night.*
The LORD will keep you from all harm—
*   he will watch over your life;*
the LORD will watch over your coming
*   and going*
*   both now and forevermore.*

Psalm 122 A Song of Ascents. Of David.

I rejoiced with those who said to me,
*   "Let us go to the house of the LORD."*
Our feet are standing
*   in your gates, O Jerusalem.*

Jerusalem is built like a city
    that is closely compacted together.
That is where the tribes go up,
    the tribes of the LORD,
to praise the name of the LORD
    according to the statute given to Israel.
There the thrones for judgment stand,
    the thrones of the house of David.
Pray for the peace of Jerusalem:
    "May those who love you be secure.
May there be peace within your walls
    and security within your citadels."
For the sake of my brothers and friends,
    I will say, "Peace be within you."
For the sake of the house of the LORD our
        God,
    I will seek your prosperity.

Psalm 48 A Song. A Psalm of the Sons of Korah.

Great is the LORD, and most worthy of
        praise,
    in the city of our God, his holy mountain.
It is beautiful in its loftiness,
    the joy of the whole earth.
Like the utmost heights of Zaphon [1] is Mount
        Zion,
    the [2] city of the Great King.
God is in her citadels;
    he has shown himself to be her fortress.
When the kings joined forces,
    when they advanced together,
they saw her and were astounded;
    they fled in terror.

Trembling seized them there,
pain like that of a woman in labor.
You destroyed them like ships of Tarshish
shattered by an east wind.
As we have heard
so have we seen
in the city of the LORD Almighty,
in the city of our God:
God makes her secure forever.
Within your temple, O God,
we meditate on your unfailing love.
Like your name, O God,
your praise reaches to the ends of the earth;
your right hand is filled with
righteousness.
Mount Zion rejoices,
the villages of Judah are glad
because of your judgments.
Walk about Zion, go around her,
count her towers.
consider well her ramparts,
view her citadels,
that you may tell of them to the next
generation.
For this God is our God for ever and ever;
he will be our guide even to the end.

1. *Zaphon* can refer to a sacred mountain or the direction north.
2. Or *earth, Mount Zion, on the northern side of the*

Psalm 126 A Song of Ascents.

When the LORD brought back the captives
to [1] Zion,
we were like men who dreamed. [2]

Our mouths were filled with laughter,
our tongues with songs of joy.
Then it was said among the nations,
"The LORD has done great things for
them."
The LORD has done great things for us,
and we are filled with joy.
Restore our fortunes, [3] O LORD,
like streams in the Negev.
Those who sow in tears
will reap with songs of joy.
He who goes out weeping,
carrying seed to sow,
will return with songs of joy,
carrying sheaves with him.

1. Or *Lord restored the fortunes of*
2. Or *men restored to health*
3. Or *Bring back our captives*

Psalm 148

Praise the LORD. [1]
Praise the LORD from the heavens,
praise him in the heights above.
Praise him, all his angels,
praise him, all his heavenly hosts.
Praise him, sun and moon,
praise him, all you shining stars.
Praise him, you highest heavens,
and you waters above the skies.
Let them praise the name of the LORD,
for he commanded and they were created.
He set them in place for ever and ever;
he gave a decree that will never pass away.

Praise the LORD from the earth,
*   you great sea creatures and all ocean depths,*
lightning and hail, snow and clouds,
*   stormy winds that do his bidding,*
you mountains and all hills,
*   fruit trees and all cedars.*
wild animals and all cattle,
*   small creatures and flying birds,*
kings of the earth and all nations,
*   you princes and all rulers on earth,*
young men and maidens,
*   old men and children.*
Let them praise the name of the LORD,
*   for his name alone is exalted;*
*   his splendor is above the earth and the*
*   heavens.*
He has raised up for his people a horn, [2]
*   the praise of all his saints,*
*   of Israel, the people close to his heart.*
Praise the LORD.

1. Hebrew *Hallelu Yah;* also in verse 14.
2. *Horn* here symbolizes strong one, that is, king.

Psalm 104:10–26

He makes springs pour water into the ravines;
*   it flows between the mountains.*
They give water to all the beasts of the
*   field;*
*   the wild donkeys quench their thirst.*
The birds of the air nest by the waters;
*   they sing among the branches.*
He waters the mountains from his upper
*   chambers;*
*   the earth is satisfied by the fruit of his work.*

He makes grass grow for the cattle,
and plants for man to cultivate—
bringing forth food from the earth:
wine that gladdens the heart of man,
oil to make his face shine,
and bread that sustains his heart.
The trees of the LORD are well watered,
the cedars of Lebanon that he planted.
There the birds make their nests;
the stork has its home in the pine trees.
The high mountains belong to the wild goats;
the crags are a refuge for the coneys. [1]
The moon marks off the seasons,
the sun knows when to go down.
You bring darkness, it becomes night,
and all the beasts of the forest prowl.
The lions roar for their prey
and seek their food from God.
The sun rises, and they steal away;
they return and lie down in their dens.
Then man goes out to his work,
to his labor until evening.
How many are your works, O LORD!
In wisdom you made them all;
the earth is full of your creatures.
There is the sea, vast and spacious,
teeming with creatures beyond number—
living things both large and small.
There the ships go to and fro,
and the leviathan, which you formed to
frolic there.

1. That is, the hyrax or rock badger

Psalm 84 For the Director of Music. According to
gittith. [1] Of the Sons of Korah. A Psalm.

How lovely is your dwelling place,
  O LORD Almighty!
My soul yearns, even faints
  for the courts of the LORD;
my heart and my flesh cry out
  for the living God.
Even the sparrow has found a home,
  and the swallow a nest for herself,
  where she may have her young—
a place near your altar,
  O LORD Almighty, my King and my God.
Blessed are those who dwell in your house;
  they are ever praising you.
Blessed are those whose strength is in you,
  who have set their hearts on pilgrimage.
As they pass through the Valley of Baca,
  they make it a place of springs;
  the autumn rains also cover it with pools. [2]
They go from strength to strength
  till each appears before God in Zion.
Hear my prayer, O LORD God Almighty;
  listen to me, O God of Jacob.
Look upon our shield, [3] O God;
  look with favor on your anointed one.
Better is one day in your courts
  than a thousand elsewhere;
  I would rather be a doorkeeper in the house of
    my God
  than dwell in the tents of the wicked.
For the LORD God is a sun and shield;
  the LORD bestows favor and honor;

no good thing does he withhold
  from those whose walk is blameless.
O LORD Almighty,
  blessed is the man who trusts in you.

1. Probably a musical term
2. Or *blessings*
3. Or *sovereign*

NOTES

1. Huston Smith, *The Religions of Man* (New York: Harper & Row, 1958) 298.

2. Adonai is the pronunciation of the four Hebrew letters that are the biblical spelling of God's name.

3. James Hastings, ed., *Dictionary of Christ and the Gospels* (Edinburgh: T. & T. Chark; New York: Scribners, 1906) 591.

4. Josephus, Flavius, *The Jewish War,* Gaalya Cornfeld, ed. (Grand Rapids, Mich.: Zondervan Publishing House, 1982) Chap. 8, 7.

5. As quoted to a group of visiting clergy in a speech in Jerusalem by Professor P. Peli of Hebrew University on March 14, 1984.

6. Alan Mairson, "Jerusalem," in *National Geographic* (April 1996), 2.

FOR FURTHER READING

Brainie, Bronwyn. *My Jerusalem* (Toronto: Doubleday, 1994).

Elon, Amos. *Jerusalem, City of Mirrors* (Boston: Little Brown, 1989).

Endo, Shusako. *A Life of Jesus* (Mahwah, N.J.: Paulist Press, 1979).

Friedman, Thomas L. *From Beruit to Jerusalem* (New York: Anchor, Doubleday, 1990).

Josephus, Flavius. *The Jewish War* (Grand Rapids, Mich.: Zondervan, 1982).

Michener, James. *The Source* (New York: Random House, 1965).

INDEX OF PLACES